CAPTURING
HEAD & HEART

CAPTURING HEAD & HEART

The Lives of Early Popular Stone-Campbell Movement Leaders

DONALD M. KINDER

LEAFWOOD Heritage

CAPTURING HEAD AND HEART

The Lives of Early Popular
Stone-Campbell Movement Leaders

LEAFWOOD Heritage

ISBN 978-0-89112-316-3
LCCN 2012008688

Printed in the United States of America

LIBRARY OF CONGRESS CATALOGING-IN-PUBLICATION DATA
Kinder, Donald Michael.
Capturing head and heart : the lives of early popular Stone-Campbell movement leaders / Donald M. Kinder.
p. cm.
Includes bibliographical references and index.
ISBN 978-0-89112-316-3 (alk. paper)
1. Restoration movement (Christianity)--Biography. I. Title.
BX7341.K56 2012
286.6092'2--dc23
[B]

2012008688

Cover design by Rick Gibson
Interior text design by Sandy Armstrong

Leafwood Publishers
1626 Campus Court
Abilene, Texas 79601
1-877-816-4455 toll free

For current information about all Leafwood titles, visit our website:
www.leafwoodpublishers.com

This volume is humbly dedicated to a true earthly saint,
Annie May Lewis.
Prior to her leaving this life, her words constantly encouraged me
and reminded me of the importance of this project.
I eagerly look forward to the day when we can meet again,
and I can say, "I finished it."

FOREWORD

Several years ago I wrote a piece on "Right-Brained Christians in a Left-Brained Church." One of my assumptions was that until somewhere about the 1970s, Churches of Christ tended to attract "left-brained" people because the DNA of our movement was shaped by "left-brained" thinkers, And I further assumed that, in recent decades, some of the children of the heritage—born with "right-brain" wiring and thus longing for more of the experiential in Christian expression—began migrating out of their left-brained heritage into to more right-brained fellowships.

However, in this book, Don Kinder tells another side of the story that has me re-thinking my assumptions. Indeed, our Restoration fathers were children of the Enlightenment and somewhat influenced by the perspectives of rationalist John Locke. And some of them may well have been left brainers—"persons of the head." But that does not necessarily mean they were not also "persons of the heart."

Kinder identifies six formative characters of the Stone-Campbell movement: Alexander Campbell, Barton Stone, Walter Scott, John Rogers, "Racoon" John Smith, and Jacob Creath Jr. He writes two sections on each: One section provides an overview of the person's life and ministry; a second section delves into the "right-brain" features of their lives. He quotes from numerous letters and articles that put the reader in touch with the hearts of these powerful intellects. In the process he leaves little doubt that these were indeed also persons of rich experience and passionate heart. In fact, it could be argued that much of what passes for "spiritual renewal" among their modern critics may pale by comparison to the nuanced passion and depth of the heart in some of our forefathers. While reading Kinder's quotes from these pioneer leaders, I found myself experiencing some of what Richard Hughes describes when he says, "On many days, I read the written witness these men had left behind and found myself stunned, simply unable to read further. On many days, my reading of these texts was as much a devotional exercise as anything else, for I found myself edified beyond measure. . . " (p. 179). Kinder then briefly explores some of the shifting currents in the movement and in the culture that seemed, at least for a time, to have swept both the head and the heart of the movement into shallower places.

This book moves us back toward a more balanced view of our nineteenth-century forebears. But far more importantly, the author here calls out for a richer balance of thoughtful theological reflection and passionate spirituality in the churches of our day. I feel confident that a great many readers will join me in expressing deep gratitude for this helpful and refreshing volume.

So dive in and read. You'll be glad you did.

Dr. Lynn Anderson
Hope Network Ministries
San Antonio, Texas

CONTENTS

Introduction 11
Capturing Head and Heart

1. **Alexander Campbell** 27
The Implementer

2. **Barton Stone** 57
Seeker of the Polar Star

3. **Walter Scott** 87
Voice of the Golden Oracle

4. **John Rogers** 113
Preacher on Horseback

5. **"Raccoon" John Smith** 137
Unifier of All Lights

6 **Jacob Creath, Jr.** 155
Contender for the Faith

7. **Conclusion** 175
The Balance of Head and Heart

Introduction

CAPTURING HEAD AND HEART

Churches of Christ, those groups along one path of the Stone-Campbell movement, are variously known by outsiders. In many circles they are known for being a people of the book — for quoting Scripture frequently in their messages. In the not-too-distant past, they were known for aggressive evangelism. They shared pride in being one of the fastest growing movements in mid-twentieth-century America. They were also known in many sectors for a rugged exclusivism. This, of course, led many an outsider to comment, "Oh, the Church of Christ, I've heard of them. Aren't they the ones who . . . ?" Those of us, like this author, who grew up inside the movement knew which phrase was often supplied. The phrase was usually anything but "deep committed spirituality" or "heartfelt piety." Head knowledge was often more accepted and more highly elevated than the heart with its deceptive emotions.

People outside the movement do not generally think of Churches of Christ as a praying people, as a spiritual people, even though there have been some giants of piety who have walked among us. One reason for this oversight in understanding could be that these "giants" just took the words of Jesus seriously when he said, "Beware of practicing your piety before men in order to be seen by them." Or could it be that there were other things going on in the movement that caught people's attention instead? Near the end of the 1990s, the *Christian Chronicle* published the findings of a major research project entitled, "Ministers' Beliefs: A Significant New Study by the Center for Church Enrichment."[1] The report had surveyed ministers of Churches of Christ around the country on key theological, social, and political positions. Interestingly, nothing was surveyed concerning spirituality, piety, devotion, or prayer.

One of the frequent charges leveled against early Stone-Campbell leaders is that they were caught up in the rationalism of the Enlightenment and the Baconian exegetical model. According to Richard Hughes, Baconianism was an eighteenth-century philosophical perspective based upon the assumption that human beings, by exercising their common sense, can know reality precisely as it is, with full confidence in the accuracy of the knowledge.[2] Sir Francis Bacon favored beginning fresh with the raw facts gathered by the five senses and then building upon those facts until truly reasonable and reliable conclusions could be reached.[3] In fact, many Christians in antebellum America were embracing the Baconian perspective, all insisting that the scientific method could unlock even biblical truths with scientific precision.[4] After all, they believed, the Bible is a perfect sourcebook of facts and any reasoning person could understand it as a logical system. The heart and the warmer emotions, as a result, fell victim to a message of salvation which called for a logical, rational response of the mind to a clear set of principles. Some suspect that this had been the specific trademark of Churches of Christ ever since. Archibald MacLean, in an interesting description of Alexander Campbell's preaching, noted that there was "no appeal to passion, no effect at pathos, no figures of rhetoric, but a warm, kindling, heated, glowing, manly argument, silencing the will, captivating the judgment, and satisfying the reason."[5]

However, even in 1901, A. B. Jones, one of the early analyzers of this movement, revealed that the restorers had a warmer, spiritual side to them. Jones wrote in his work, *The Spiritual Side of Our Plea*,

"A restoration of original apostolic Christianity, in letter and in spirit, was their motto."[6] Indeed, as one peers closer into this restoration heritage, one finds a deeply committed, even heartfelt, spirituality in several of the forefathers in the faith. Even Alexander Campbell, who so many have claimed bequeathed to subsequent generations the rational, emotionally deficient worship, was an individual of tremendous faith, warmth, and humor. To be clear, he never thought that one's conversion was something spooky or mysterious. Indeed, it was all explicable by the Holy Spirit's use of arguments addressed to the mind to bring sinners to right relationship with God.[7] He felt that the heart was not a reliable guide to spirituality. He wrote in 1829, "If operations, impulses or feelings, were to be the basis of our conviction, it would be founding the most important of all knowledge upon the most uncertain of all foundations. 'The heart of man is deceitful above all things,' . . . He that trusts in his own heart is a fool."[8] He summarized his assertions with the declaration, "I walk by faith, not by feelings."[9]

Nevertheless, Campbell could still be a man of intense prayer and private devotion, a man of deep, heart-felt piety. Carisse Berryhill even argues that Campbell's eloquence of speech was more than just to inform the understanding, but was also to delight the imagination, move the passions, and persuade the will.[10]

Coming out of Scotch Presbyterian background, both father Thomas and Alexander were believers in family devotions and daily prayer. Back in Ireland, before the family migrated to America, Thomas would preside over the morning and evening prayers and Bible reading. Thomas then sailed to America first and asked the family to join him later. Within a year the family followed father Thomas to the New World. But even during the passage on the ship, without the father present, the mother would call all the members into the room and Alexander would lead them, morning and evening, in their prayers and private devotions.

The morning and evening plan of family devotions would continue throughout Alexander's life. Twice a day in his own family, he would gather the family members in the dining room where he would lead them in worship. When his preaching tours took him away from home, his wife Selena would take the lead in this faith-building service. Wycliffe Campbell, Alexander's eleven-year-old son, had memorized the first fourteen chapters of Proverbs, as well as a number of hymns. Before his tragic drowning, he had planned to quote these to his father upon his father's return from the British Isles preaching tour.[11] In 1832, Alexander Campbell satirized Christians who thought they did not need to pray more than once a week.[12]

Some of Campbell's most beautiful thoughts on prayer are when he discusses those secret, quiet moments with the Lord. He wrote that the best school "under heaven" to learn prayer is really not classroom instruction but time in one's closet, in fields, in forests, "where no human ear can hear us, no human eye can see us."[13] These secret prayers, he believed, are the ones that influence us the most.

Campbell felt that the Christian's heart should be visible on his face and in his conduct. He believed that if one's heart were pure, warm, and full of devout affections, then the outward person should naturally display the inner one. Furthermore, Campbell was convinced that body language was part of worship. Prayer posture meant something. In 1835 he noted that people who stay seated and address God do not glorify him. He reminded people that in prayer one is addressing the Lord Almighty.[14] He returned to the topic again in 1845, as he discussed prayers in the assembly. He wrote in his *Millennial Harbinger* that when people offer prayers in church, "kneeling should be preferred, when it could be made convenient." Kneeling was a sign of submission before the One who is much higher than one's self.[15]

Barton Stone, the other early giant in the movement, whose followers merged with the Campbell movement in 1832, was known widely for his humble Christ-like character and his attention to the heart, as well as his constant devotion to prayer. In his autobiography Stone wrote that even when he was quite young he "had been in the habit of retiring in secret, morning and evening, for prayer."[16] While Stone is known for his association with the extreme emotionalism and unusual manifestations of the Spirit at the Cane Ridge revival in 1801, he himself was never perceptively affected by the "bodily exercises." He was sympathetic to them and rejoiced that people by the hundreds were turning to the Lord. At the same time, he knew that many could boast about receiving the Spirit but all the while be destitute of it. He said that one might ask of the claimants, "Do they pray in secret, and with their families night and morning? If not, is not their religion vain? Is it better than infidels?"[17]

In Stone's later years, as his age and illnesses led him to an awareness that his term of service would soon be ending, he wrote a series of articles from an "Old Preacher to a Young Preacher." He told the young evangelists: "Be holy out of the pulpit as in it . . . . Be often on your knees, always endeavor to keep God before your mind, and labor to please him, rather than man."[18]

Stone, like Campbell, felt that prayer posture was taken far too lightly in church service. He wrote in his *Christian Messenger* that he had seen too common everywhere the "indecent mode of the congregation's worship in prayer. Some were kneeling, others sitting, and others standing in time of prayer." Stone realized that there were indeed cases in which a congregation could not kneel, as for example, when a great crowd was present, but he wrote that "few cases can justify the posture of sitting." He wondered if the reason that more did not kneel was because they were fearful of dirtying their fine garments. Stone had the answer: "This pretext should be removed by having the floors of the houses clean." Stone believed that there is "hardly a more serious sight on earth, than to see a congregation kneeling in prayer before their God."[19]

Walter Scott, the other of the big four of the early leaders, after Thomas and Alexander Campbell, and Barton Stone, worked as an evangelist in Northeast Ohio, baptizing a thousand per year from

1827-1830. Before he accepted the assignment to evangelize the Western Reserve,[20] he spent two months in prayer and study, and in consultation with fellow believers. His preaching would then encompass messages two or three times daily, traveling constantly on horseback, sleeping and eating wherever he could.[21] Part of his method would involve talking to children on the playground, and having them memorize five steps to salvation on their fingers. He would then tell the children to run home and tell their parents to come out that night and hear him talk about those steps. Houses would be packed to overflowing. Scott's message was clear and simple. People remembered his sermons twenty years later.

Yet, for Scott, conversion was always more than just a matter of how one aligned facts in the head. He would often accompany another preacher on a tour and both men would address a crowd at the meeting. On the way to one such appointment, Scott would say to the younger preacher, "Now I will tell you how we must do: I will preach, and you must follow in an exhortation; I will strike at the head, and you must strike at the heart."[22] Conversion always involved one's total being.

Scott also loved to be with the Lord in nature. Scott worked in that part of Western Pennsylvania and Ohio that is still replete with hills and forests. He loved to climb to the tops of the hills, away from the city and commune with his beautiful God of nature. For Scott, nature as well as the Word could reveal divinity. Walking with one of his students, Robert Richardson, in a garden outside the classroom on one occasion, he picked up a rose and handed it to him and said, "Do you know why Scripture calls Jesus the Rose of Sharon?" Robert could think of no reply. Scott surveyed again the delicate flower, and looked at Robert and said, "It's because this particular rose has no thorns. It is utter, unblemished beauty"—just like Jesus. He saw Jesus as the center of all Scripture and all doctrine. He saw himself as the voice of that "golden oracle."

Scott was enraptured with the message of Scripture. He encouraged every head of every household to spend time memorizing the

Word of God. He wrote: "A chapter a day will put the head of a family in possession of the entire New Testament in much less than one year, for there are only 260 chapters in the volume."[23] Scott put his own advice into practice. He would often finish in the classroom, and then be busy until midnight, studying, learning, and memorizing the text.

Other early Stone-Campbell leaders seemed just as zealous for the work as the "Big Four" and just as committed to letting the Lord capture both head and heart. They knew that by themselves they were not up to the task. "Raccoon" John Smith carried his Bible with him to the field and kept it beside his plate when he ate. Jacob Creath, Jr. was known to walk a mile after breakfast daily to a nearby grove, where he would concentrate on his messages and commit himself to God in prayer. Creath would begin every New Year by reading Genesis 1, and would complete the Bible by the year's end. He continued this practice for fifty years. James Garfield, who was a successful preacher before his success in the military and politics, read the Bible daily. Often he read the Bible at sunset, because his mother had told him that was when she would also be reading the Scriptures. Isaac Errett, editor of the *Christian Standard*, once remarked, "With the help of God, I will rise at 4 o'clock each morning and spend until 6 in reading the Bible and in prayer."[24] J. W. McGarvey, long-time teacher and preacher, preferred not to read from the Bible either in the pulpit or in the classroom. Instead, he always quoted every passage from memory. David and Margaret Lipscomb held their family devotionals at 9 p.m. daily and always invited their guests to participate. W. L. Karnes said of James A. Harding, "Harding caused more people to read their Bibles than any man for the past fifty years."[25]

However, as the movement moved across America, not all remained focused on heart as well as mind. After Scott had been preaching for a few decades, he began to notice that too many people were beginning their days without prayer and that families were neglecting the practice of daily family study. He said that there were "thousands who never think of such a matter, and this is not the worst of it. There are professing populations of one thousand in which there is not a family that calls upon the Lord night and morning." He challenged the movement, "Let us be a prayerful people and a praying people; let us be full of the spirit of praise."[26] Scott believed that when people returned to meeting God on a daily basis, God would indeed bless them with more blessings than they could hold[27]

Not only could one's careful, as well as prayerful, balance of mind and heart get pushed aside by the cares of the world, but Barton Stone and others wrote that sometimes the prideful quest for purer doctrine dampened personal spirituality and devotion to God. Stone believed that one should definitely know doctrine and how to defend it. Head cannot be neglected. Yet, Stone witnessed that the years had brought a different spirit into the movement. He expressed with sadness: "Now people are saying in their defense of doctrines, never to yield on one point, or submit to one argument, however just and plain." Unlike the earlier days of the movement when prayer and devotion filled people's attention, Stone complained that now

> the hours set apart for meditation and secret prayer are neglected, or, if attended to, are interrupted, and the thoughts of the heart are diverted to these divisive doctrines, how they can be established or overthrown to advantage. When the Scriptures are read, it is not to hold converse with God, to learn duty and do it, but to find something there to establish their received doctrines of controversy. When the pulpit is ascended, the burden of the sermon is the agitated controversies of the day, teaching the congregation the art of war.[28]

According to Stone, within a generation, attention and energy began to be focused on maintaining true doctrine. Others coming into the movement wanted assurance that truth was not being compromised.

Richard Hughes contends that it was Campbell who inaugurated the tradition of debates in Churches of Christ that lasted for generations.[29] Leroy Brownlow challenged the idea that debates ever dominated the movement. He argued that there were always more gospel meetings than debates through this period, and thus we never lost sight of evangelism.[30] Nevertheless, Barton Stone himself noted the effect of the debating spirit. Stone warned that "debates tend to strife, deaden piety, destroy the spirit of prayer, puff up the vain mind."[31] In other words, as the size of heads increased, hearts definitely diminished. In 1844, near the end of his life, Stone complained that many of his own people increasingly placed biblical knowledge, religious controversy, and debate over "godliness, piety and brotherly love." He asked: "Do we see genuine Christianity promoted by such controversies and debates? Look around and enquire for these fruits? Do you know of any person spiritually renewed or refreshed with spiritual understanding? Do you find brotherly love and Christian union advanced? On the contrary, do you not find their opposites promoted?"[32]

William Lipscomb, who began the *Gospel Advocate* with Tolbert Fanning, wrote in 1856:

> In the midst of the fierce and unscrupulous warfare with which the movement called the Reformation of the 19th c. has been forced to contend, there, no doubt, has been too little attention given to the solemn and imperative duties of the Christian profession. The exertions which have been made, have been directed more to the exposure of the delusion of others, and to the defense of the gospel as God's only authority for the guidance of man, than to the noble and heavenly culture of the Christian life . . . . The Christian religion has never been made the first great matter of life. Its interests and concerns have been secondary. We have not permitted it to sink into our hearts, and fix itself in our affections as the great controlling and guiding influence of our lives. We are not as truly godly and devoted as we need to be . . . . My brethren, what could

> we not do in Tennessee if we were a God-fearing and God-trusting people? We have given ourselves to him only in part.[33]

Robert Richardson, who authored the *Memoirs of Alexander Campbell*, wrote: "Too many people are ready to argue, debate, discuss, at all time . . . and will spend hours in the earnest defense of their favorite themes, but will not spend five minutes meditating upon the character, the sayings, and perfections of Christ, or upon their own inward state."[34] Leonard Allen refers to Richardson as an oasis of spirituality in a time when "heartless and superficial formalism" was overtaking the movement.[35] Richardson believed that the debating mindset was producing a deadly spiritual vacuum. The net effect of doctrinal controversy, he felt, would be to "distract the mind, destroy love, generate dislike, jealousy, revenge [and] foster the passions of the carnal nature."[36] Unlike others of his time,[37] he refused to concede that the Spirit's work was limited to the facts of the gospel message contained in a first-century document. Natural theology is also a work of the Spirit. While nature cannot bring a sinner to repentance, it surely brings one closer to the Creator. The Spirit is also moving in the spheres of divine proclamation, and is instrumental in God's responses to prayers.[38]

John Rogers, who helped promote the union of the Stone and Campbell movements, cites another possible reason for a reduction in heart. Rogers had written to Alexander in 1834: "Many of us, in running away from the extreme of enthusiasm, have, on the other hand, passed the temperate zone, and gone far into the frozen regions . . . . There is in too many churches, a cold-hearted, lifeless formality that freezes the energies."[39] Perhaps the fear of the excesses of the pervasive revival mentality drove some to a more rational, and in Rogers' estimation, a colder experience of faith.

The twenty-first century has witnessed a renewed emphasis on heart-felt spirituality and worship. This renewed look at these neglected aspects of the Christian faith is being felt not only among Churches of

Christ, but in wider circles as well. As last century drew to a close, one author in the tenth anniversary issue of *Image* magazine (1995) wrote: "Never in my lifetime have I seen people as interested in matters of worship as they have been in the past few years. We seem especially focused on finding ways to encounter God in worship and appropriate forms of praising him as we do." The author continued: "Prayer has become a greater part of our personal and corporate lives. We hear more about seeking God's will and the leading of his spirit than at any other time I can remember. Groups and individuals are committing themselves to periods of prayer, fasting and meditation, and other spiritual disciplines."[40]

Around the country, Christian retreats are now being held whose sole purpose is praise. Churches plan worship weekends for their praise teams so they can better lead in public worship.[41] Books of a devotional character are among every Christian bookstore's best sellers. Notice the immense popularity of the books of Max Lucado, not only within Stone-Campbell circles, but throughout evangelical Christianity. He is now called "America's Pastor." Yet, his successful style definitely highlights heart more than head, thoroughly unlike many of his movement's predecessors. Two of the more recent Harding School of Theology Ministry Forums have dealt with worship.[42] People in various denominations are deliberately giving more attention to worship and trying to rejuvenate their own relationship with the Lord. Transformational churches are now about the business of the makeover of the whole person. Tremper Longman III's recent volume on *Reading the Bible with Heart and Mind* endeavors to instruct one how to read the Bible not only for intellectual knowledge, but for spiritual transformation.[43] The *Stone Campbell Journal*, which saw its inception near the turn of the century, sought "a restoration of mind to heart."[44]

The chapters that follow will look at six of the early Stone-Campbell movement leaders, seeking to rediscover their hearts as well as minds. Past biographers of these individuals tended to focus on the aspects that promoted certain contemporary agendas or controversies. The resulting images of these influential leaders were too often cold and irrelevant to anything beyond boundary issues.

I recognize that the word "heart" is nearly as slippery as the word "love." Perhaps the "heart" that we want to explore here is what is currently acknowledged in the controversial right brain/left brain research. Models that base themselves on the initial research of Roger Sperry in the 1960s usually posit that the left hemisphere assists one in the control of verbal skills and processes information in the form of analytical and chronological ways. It looks at all available pieces, then puts them together to form the entire image.[45] Research from the University of Indiana also contends that the left-brain is the rational side of the person—it seeks plan and structure, prefers established, certain information, and controls feelings.[46] In some ways, this is an apt description of where the Stone-Campbell movement has lived much of the past two hundred years.

The right hemisphere of the brain, however, in Indiana's assessment, is intuitive, fluid and spontaneous, and free with feelings.[47] Other models reveal that right-brained individuals are usually more creative and drawn to the arts and music.[48] This is clearly not an assessment of most of those in the Stone-Campbell camp.

Admittedly, no individual is completely left or right brain, and both hemispheres within the brain possess many mutual connections. Nevertheless, studies show that a person is usually dominated by one hemisphere or the other. Researchers such as Eric Jensen have contributed useful explorations into how awareness of left-brain/right-brain dominance assists in teaching and learning methodology.[49]

This book, while acknowledging our past left-brain tendencies, calls us to take another look at those among us who at least occasionally wandered into right brain activities of the "heart." The scheme in this author's re-telling will be to first summarize the individual's life, concentrating on those events that shaped both his career and his character. This will be followed by an analysis of what can be known of the more hidden inner life and thought. I contend that Alexander Campbell, Barton Stone, Walter Scott, John Rogers, "Raccoon" John Smith, and Jacob Creath, Jr. were all flesh and blood whose "hearts" need to be shared once again. For those seeking spiritual renewal, one that surrounds both head and heart, these figures in the past cannot be neglected. Finally, for anyone searching for methods to rejuvenate contemporary worship, whether in private or in the corporate assembly, these voices reclaimed from history can still speak. My only wish is to make their words clear enough that we will want to listen.

Introduction Notes

1. Mel Hailey, Doug Foster, and Thomas Winter, "Ministers' Beliefs," *Christian Chronicle* (July, 1996): 15-17.

2. Richard Hughes, *Reviving the Ancient Faith: The Story of Churches of Christ in America* (1996; 2nd edition, Abilene, Tex.: Abilene Christian University Press), 31.

3. See John C. Nugent, "Was Alexander Campbell Enslaved to Scottish Baconianism?" *Stone Campbell Journal* 12 (Spring, 2009): 15-30. Nugent concludes that Campbell's debt to Scottish Baconianism has been exaggerated, and rather than being enslaved to such philosophy, was driven instead by more eschatological and ecumenical concerns.

4. Timothy Sensing, "Baconian Method and Preaching in the Stone-Campbell Movement," *Stone Campbell Journal* 4 (Fall, 2001): 163-64.

5. Archibald McLean, *Alexander Campbell as a Preacher* (St. Louis: Christian Publications, 1908), 25.

6. A. B. Jones, *The Spiritual Side of Our Plea* (St. Louis: Christian Publications, 1901), 69.

7. Max Ward Randall, *The Great Awakenings and the Restoration Movement* (Joplin, Mo.: College Press, 1983), 360.

8. Alexander Campbell, "A Catalogue of Queries-Answered," *Christian Baptist* 6 (2 February, 1829): 166.

9. Ibid.

10. Carisse Mickey Berryhill, "Alexander Campbell's Natural Rhetoric of Evangelism," *Restoration Quarterly* 30 (1980): 112. Sensing argues for the clear methodological intent of Campbell's sermons. Usually he began with the persuasive marshalling of evidence to support the testimony of Scripture. Then, after the proofs were presented, the preacher could encourage the audience by appealing to the emotions. This appeal to feelings is only proper after the audience is first convinced by the facts. Sensing, "Baconian Method," 181.

11. Dabney Phillips, *A Medley of the Restoration* (Montgomery, Ala.: Bible & School Supply, 1978), 39.

12. Alexander Campbell, *Millennial Harbinger* 3 (1832): 64.

13. Ibid., 498.

14. Ibid. (1835): 488-89.

15. Ibid., "Church Organization," *Millennial Harbinger* 3rd series, no. 2 (1845): 66.

16. John Rogers, *The Biography of Eld. Barton Warren Stone* (Cincinnati: J.A. & U. P. James, 1847), 5.

17. Barton Stone, *Christian Messenger* 10 (1836): 20.

18. Quoted in James Madison Mathes, *Works of Elder B. W. Stone, to which is added a few discourses and sermons* (Cincinnati: Moore, Witstach, Keys & Co., 1859), 343.

19. Barton Stone, *Christian Messenger* 13 (1843): 168.

20. Northeastern Ohio.

21. Phillips, *A Medley of the Restoration*, 70.

22. William Baxter, *Life of Elder Walter Scott* (Nashville: Gospel Advocate, nd), 257.

23. Dwight Stevenson, *Walter Scott: Voice of the Golden Oracle* (Joplin, Mo.: College Press, 1946), 140.

24. Phillips, *A Medley of the Restoration*, 71.

25. Ibid., 40.

26. Barton Stone, "Non-Worship Families," *Christian Evangelist* (April, 1840): 89- 90.

27. Ibid., 109.

28. Quoted in Mathes, *Works of Elder B. W. Stone*, 210f.

29. Hughes, *Reviving the Ancient Faith*, 105.

30. Leroy Brownlow, "Review of Some of the Assertions and Charges in the 'The Worldly Church,'" *Firm Foundation* 106 (April 1, 1991): 16.

31. Quoted in Hughes, *Reviving the Ancient Faith*, 105.

32. Ibid.

33. William Lipscomb, "Are We a Devoted People?" *Gospel Advocate* (1856): 136ff.

34. Quoted in Leonard Allen, *Distant Voices: Discovering a Forgotten Past for a Changing Church* (Abilene, Tex.: ACU Press, 1993), 65.

35. Ibid., 66.

36. Ibid., 65.

37. Richardson branded Fanning, editor of the *Gospel Advocate*, as an illustration of the "Word only" approach. Fanning's response was to brand Richardson a "spiritualist" in the same camp with the wild Nashville minister, Jesse Ferguson. Steve Singleton, "Robert Richardson on the Holy Spirit: Balance

between Rationalism and Spiritualism," *Stone Campbell Journal* 1.2 (Fall, 1998): 161.

38. Ibid., 160. See also Robert Richardson, *A Scriptural View of the Office of the Holy Spirit* (Cincinnati: Bosworth, Chase & Hall, 1873).

39. Allen, *Distant Voices*, 79.

40. Jeanene Reese, "Reflections on an Anniversary," *Image* 11 (July 1, 1995): 18.

41. The Church of Christ at White Station, Memphis, Tennessee, participates with other area churches in this event annually.

42. 1997 Forum, "Experiencing Meaningful Worship," and 1994, "Styles of Worship in Churches of Christ Today."

43. Tremper Longman III, *Reading the Bible with Heart and Mind* (Colorado Springs, Colo.: NavPress, 1997).

44. Editor's preface, *Stone Campbell Journal* 1 (Spring, 1998): 3.

45. See http:///www.healthandsoul.com

46. http://www.indiana.edu/~reading/ieo/bibs/left.html

47. Ibid.

48. http://www.heraldsun.com.au/news/right-brain-v-left-brain/story-e6frf7jo-1111114603615

49. Some of his books include *Teaching with the Brain in Mind*, 2nd ed. (Association for Supervision and Curriculum Development, 1998), *Brain/Mind Learning Principles in Action* (Corwin Press, 2005), and *Brain-Based Learning: The New Paradigm in Teaching* (Crown Press, 2008).

Chapter One

ALEXANDER CAMPBELL

The Implementer

For much of the last century, if someone were to ask the question, "For what are Churches of Christ famous?" the typical responses would have included the following: "They are a people based on the Bible," "Their preachers quote scriptures in their sermons," "They like to argue," or "They are the people who think they are the only ones going to heaven." Rarely has a response been: "They are a people of heart-felt prayer" or "Those people have a great devotional life." Admittedly, that has not been the image they have presented. Yet many in their fellowship have been great men and women of prayer. Perhaps it has been in the quest for truth, and the claim to be right that the core of what it really means to be a follower of Jesus has been forgotten. At its core is not just knowing truth, but knowing the Lord who is truth. He said in John 14:6, "I am the way, the truth and the life."

At the same time, there have been many in this branch of the Stone-Campbell heritage who were, in fact, people of great faith. They knew truth and knew the Lord, and had private devotional lives of which many knew nothing. Yet those who examined and reported on this history in the past two hundred years have too often employed selective memories, stating that this heritage originated in those captivated by the proper alignment of head knowledge only. It has been stated that these preachers and fathers of the church more than a century ago became overly rational and overly legalistic in their presentation of the message. These individuals had no place for heart-felt religion. In some sectors it was reported that there was a theological battle of brothers, between the emotional Barton Stone of Kentucky and the rational Alexander Campbell of Virginia. In the end the "Campbellites" won.

In this new twenty-first century, many are again scrutinizing this heritage and deciding afresh what things needs to remain and what needs to be cast aside. It is appropriate, therefore, to look again at its early leaders and study not only what they expounded, but also who they were as flesh and blood disciples of the Christ. What we discover is that these leaders have always been multi-faceted, with many sides to their personalities, even sometimes surprisingly deep and devout, emotional sides. Even Alexander Campbell, who so many have claimed gave the movement its rational worship and rational gospel presentation, was a man of unusually great faith, warmth, and humor, as well as a man of prayer and private devotion.

PART ONE: Alexander's Story (1788-1866)

Leroy Garrett stated that Thomas Campbell's "greatest gift to the movement was his son," Alexander. Father Thomas was the thinker, while the son became the implementer. It was Alexander's father who said, "We speak where the Bible speaks and we are silent where the Bible is silent." But how does that work? It would remain for the son, Alexander, to work out the practicalities of how that is done.

Scottish Heritage

As one can tell from the name, the family is of Scottish descent. The Campbells had migrated from western Scotland to Ireland about seven generations before Alexander was born. His mother was Jane, who was of French (Huguenot) Calvinist descent. Alexander's boyhood was spent in Northern Ireland, in an area about thirty or forty miles from Belfast. The surrounding countryside contains some of the most lush and green landscapes anywhere in Europe.

Alexander, the first of ten children of Jane and Thomas Campbell, was born on September 12, 1788. His early training was from his father. He grew up as a "preacher's kid," with all of the perks, privileges, and accompanying reputation.[1] Father Thomas Campbell had graduated from the University of Glasgow, and in Ireland served as a schoolmaster, preaching occasionally for a nearby Presbyterian church. It was a congregation of the Old Light, Anti-Burgher faction of the Seceder Presbyterian Church of Scotland. Practically, this meant that Alexander's family was not wealthy, but they were not destitute either. Thomas, being a Presbyterian clergyman and teacher, was a respected member of the community. On one occasion, local Lord Gosford requested Thomas to bring his family to live in the castle with him and be the private tutor for his family. It would have been an excellent career move, allowing the family to live in a castle while Thomas received a handsome salary for his work. The decision was a tough one. The older Campbell prayed and then decided "No" out of concern for children. His reasoning was that life in the castle would not be good for their spiritual upbringing. Assessing the impact of those early years, the time spent by young Alexander in Ireland clearly shaped the spirituality, as well as devotional life he would have later. It also became what he would recommend for other families.

Family devotions were presided over by father Thomas, and included morning and evening prayers and Bible reading. Thomas Campbell remembered being whipped as a child for praying too long in family worship. So, when time came to rear his own children, Thomas tried to achieve a better balance of patience and firmness. Alexander would later remember the discipline of his father as "the most perfect

I ever witnessed." He wrote, "He always honored his word. What he promised he performed, and what he threatened he executed and fulfilled to the letter."[2] Consistency paid off. Thomas gave his children assignments from the Bible, the catechism, and various classics. Many years later in his personal memoirs (1860), Alexander recounted his father's emphasis upon "living for eternity" rather than for "time alone." In those family devotionals and other times, Thomas called on his children to be prepared to give an account to God for the use they made of themselves, of their means and opportunities to do good, to be happy, and to make others happy. Later Alexander penned, "Whatever good, little or much, I may have achieved under God, I owe it all, and those who benefited by it owe it all, to his paternal care and instruction, and especially his example." To be fair, he appreciated his mother too, but he acknowledged more of his father's influence than his mother's. Nevertheless, Alexander spoke of his mother as the "most affectionate and exemplary mother." She made home, he said, a "sweet home," with "all of its fascinating charms and attractions."

Much, if not all, of Alexander's schooling was provided by his father at home.[3] He would also spend a couple of years at an academy owned by his uncle. Before he was sixteen years old, Alexander had studied Latin and Hebrew, and memorized the book of Proverbs and parts of the Psalms. This was part of Thomas' plan for all the children.

Like a typical boy, Alexander was not always studious. He loved swimming and making snowballs with his unusually large hands. He enjoyed hunting game with nets or with a dog and gun.[4] A favorite story among his biographers is the time when Alexander was nine years old and was supposed to be studying his French. He fell asleep under a tree and when he awoke the family cow had eaten half the textbook. No time passed before Thomas found out about it and scolded him, "That cow has more French in her stomach than you have in your head!"

By the time Alexander was seventeen, his inner life was in turmoil. He later described the period this way:

> From the time that I could read the Scriptures [from childhood, presumably], I became convinced that Jesus was the Son of God. I was also fully persuaded that I was a sinner, and must obtain pardon through the merits of Christ or be lost forever. This caused me great distress of soul, and I had much exercise of mind under the awakenings of a guilty conscience. Finally, after many strugglings, I was enabled to put my trust in my Savior, and to feel my reliance on him as the only Savior of sinners. From the moment I was able to feel this reliance on the Lord Jesus Christ, I obtained and enjoyed peace of mind.

Later, he would reject that subjective conversion experience for a more objective one in immersion baptism. At any rate, upon such a conversion as above, the Ahorey congregation of Ireland received the young Alexander as a member.[5] There may, in fact, have actually been a more substantial "conversion experience," though the details of it are not known. The one closest to knowing what actually happened to young Alexander was "Raccoon" John Smith, who described his conversation with Campbell as follows:

> Having crossed Licking River and riding slowly up the bank, I asked Brother Campbell to tell me *his experience*. He readily did so, and in turn asked a relation of mine, which was given. After hearing his experience, I would cheerfully have given him the hand of fellowship. It was one which any Baptist church would have cheerfully received, and was almost substantially such as mine. He took occasion to say that he had never discarded the existence of such experiences on the part of the sinner, but objected to the use made of such things, as determining the proper prerequisites of baptism, and went on to explain the necessity of taking the *word of God*, than our feelings, as guides in such things.[6]

The University of Glasgow

In 1807, for several reasons, Thomas migrated to America. For one, his doctor recommended the move for better health, not only for the prospect of a better life in general. Besides, many of his friends had traveled there already. Their plan called for the family to join the father a little later after he had made the initial preparation in the new land. Consequently, when Alexander was eighteen, his father left him in charge of the family and the academy and went on ahead to America to seek a suitable location in Pennsylvania, a place where numerous Scotch-Irish immigrants had already settled. On April 1, 1807, Alexander bade his father goodbye as Thomas boarded the *Brutus* bound for America.

It was at this point in his life that one becomes aware of the devotional side of Campbell. This was the year in which he began his journal. During this period of separation, Alexander often referred to "my mother and the children." In March of 1808, the family received a welcome letter from Thomas (dated January 1) saying that America was a "land of peace, liberty and prosperity." He urged his wife and children to "omit no opportunity of removing [themselves from Ireland], as the Lord may graciously permit." Indeed, they would have left immediately had it not been for a few problems, chief of which was an outbreak of smallpox among several of the younger children.

Finally on September 28, 1808, the Campbell clan journeyed to Londonderry and boarded the ship, *Hibernia*. Almost from the beginning of the voyage, the weather was terrible. As on land, now onboard ship, the family continued their usual family devotionals. Every early morning and evening the family would assemble and Alexander would lead them as they prayed for safe passage to America.

Unfortunately, or perhaps providentially, the journey was delayed. The ship was only two days out of port, when winds blew so strong that the crew had little choice but to anchor in an inlet on the coast of the Isle of Islay. The ship rode the anchor for three days, until it finally crashed into the rocks that lay below the waterline. Campbell's own diary described the scene:

> We set to fire our guns of distress but fired in vain. There was no human hand that could assist us nor ear to hear us for the dreadful noise of the roaring wind and waves filled the air with dreadful sounds. All the passengers came on deck where the breaking waves dashed over them. In this situation we spent the most part of that long and terrible night, a night never to be forgotten by those concerned in these terrors.

During these tense moments Alexander vowed that if God would spare his life, he would give his life to the ministry. God did spare his life. As the ship was towed back to port, all gave thanks that no lives were lost. But it was too late in the season to attempt another crossing. So, with a portion of the refund he had received from the owners of the ship, Alexander used the following months to attend his father's old alma mater in Scotland.

For more than six months Alexander studied at the University of Glasgow. Many of his essays and notes from lectures have survived. The year 1808 seems to have been especially pivotal in Alexander Campbell's spiritual development. During that time in Scotland, he came into contact with several who would help direct him towards New Testament Christianity. The influence of the Haldane brothers and Greville Ewing is a study in itself. To summarize, these were independent Scottish thinkers who had broken from the Church of Scotland and had now begun practicing congregational autonomy and weekly observance of the Lord's Supper. Alexander would bring these same ideas to America.

However, before he left Scotland, one major event would occur. It would be Alexander's own break with the Presbyterian Church of Scotland. On the evening of the Sunday in which communion would be offered to all Presbyterians, Alexander went to see the elders of the church and, according to custom, received the little token that gave permission to take the Lord's Supper the following morning. The next day, however, as he stood in the long line waiting to receive the Lord's Supper, he came to a decision. He dropped the token in the basket, but refused to take the Lord's Supper. In his own mind, this was a symbolic break with the church of his youth.

New Life in a New Country

The next year the family attempted passage to America again. As before, several storms blew across the Atlantic, but the weather for crossing had significantly improved. Aboard the ship, Alexander wrote a long poem in which he celebrated the majesty of the ocean and the goodness of the Creator. Part of it reads:

> But let us still that power, that goodness love,
> That rules o'er all below and all above;
> Each of his Creatures move at His command
> In the great sea, or on the spacious land.

One can imagine young Alexander standing on the deck of the ship with his hands clasped to the rails. As the wind blew his hair, he inhaled the fragrant salt spray. In every direction was the canvas of blue. It had to have been a powerful sight that inspired both his spirit and his writing.

Finally, the family arrived in America and began the two week trek across the mountains to the town of Washington, Pennsylvania.[7] Following the much-awaited family reunion, Alexander discovered, to his surprise, that his father had also left the Scottish Presbyterian Church. Together in America, they began the Brush Run congregation, guided by Thomas Campbell's principles in his document "The Declaration and Address." The document stated that they would make the New Testament their church constitution, rejecting creeds and confessions of faith, and follow the Scriptures only. Then, within just a few years, especially at the impetus of the birth of Alexander's first daughter, they adopted immersion of adult believers for the forgiveness of sins as the New Testament design for baptism.

On the last day of 1809, Alexander mused about the approaching year and wrote out his personal "Resolutions and Arrangements." It was to be his program for daily study and personal development.

PROPOSED DAILY SCHEDULE

	Hours
Marginal readings of the scriptures	1/2
Read Scot [Scott's Family Bible]	2
Hebrew	1/2
Greek	1/2
Latin	1/2
Poetry	1/2
Philosophy	1/2
Composition	2
	Total: 7 hrs.

—Alexander Campbell, 1809[8]

He included in his diary a prayer that "God in his great mercy" would supply the "time, ability and inclination to attend to these." Later, when he began a job as a tutor, he shortened his personal studies to a more manageable four and a half hours a day.[9]

Alexander did not write much about his wife, Margaret. He met her when he was twenty-two. He was delivering some books for his father to John Brown, about fifteen miles from Washington. During one of his book deliveries to the Brown mansion, John Brown introduced young Alexander to his wife, daughter, and stepdaughter. Robert Richardson, Campbell's earliest biographer, described Margaret as "tall and slender, but graceful. She had a sweet benignant countenance, very dark hair, regular features, full and expressive dark hazel eyes, and was already noted for her piety, industry and engaging manners."[10]

Preacher, Publisher, Debater

Alexander never took pay for his preaching. Thomas heard his son make that declaration and warned him, "My son, I fear you will have to wear many a ragged coat."[11] Alexander never did. The reason? Upon his marriage to Margaret, his new father-in-law gave him three hundred acres of property around Bethany, Virginia, with its accompanying mansion. Campbell spent the rest of his years being a rather successful breeder of sheep. He expanded his estate through land speculation in Ohio. He also published two successful journals in his lifetime, the *Christian Baptist* (seventeen years) and the *Millennial Harbinger* (nearly forty years). Both were widely read in several states—Ohio, Kentucky, Tennessee, Virginia, Illinois, and Indiana.[12]

It was during these productive years that Campbell gave shape to the movement. He participated in several public debates; some of these were nationally acclaimed. He debated with great eloquence such issues as baptism for the forgiveness of sins, the doctrines of Presbyterians and Catholics, and the existence of God against the infamous Robert Owen. Initially, he was hesitant to embrace the practice of public debate until someone convinced him that more people show up for public debates than ever appear in church on Sundays.[13]

His travels were extensive, preaching and holding meetings while raising first one family and then another. According to Margaret's instruction on her deathbed, his second marriage was to a longtime family friend, Selena. She would bear him six more children. He already had eight by Margaret. He possessed a full head of hair until his death. Selena remembered that his eyesight and hearing remained good to the end. Sometimes Alexander would smile as he remarked to Selena, "They talk loud to me because I am so gray; they think I am deaf, but I am not."[14]

He penned thousands of pages in his journals on what it means to "restore the ancient order of things." He desired that churches in his time contain people who are trying to be Christians only and nothing else. He died in 1866, having lived through the American Civil War. Perhaps there has been no one of his stature, intellect, and influence in the movement that still bears his name. But what of his heart?

PART TWO: Alexander's Heart

Campbell had a heart. Sometimes this is forgotten as one reads through his articles or works through the arguments of his famous debates. Nevertheless, one catches a glimpse of his warmer side in several places. To begin, it is found in his poetry. Campbell wrote the lyrics for several hymns. The following is taken from a love letter to his first girlfriend in America, Hannah Acheson.

> Your love can make me truly blest
> O why that bliss destroy
> Refuse me not this one request
> And great shall be my joy.

Campbell had wanted to marry her, but for whatever reason, plans changed. Later his heart re-appeared often in the beautiful, sometimes humorous love letters to his wife, Margaret, and then to his second wife, Selena.[15] "You must know," he wrote in one letter to Selena, "that I always open your epistles with palpitating heart. When I break open the seal I think of the fingers that made it secure and of the heart that is sealed to me, and that it is open to me as mine is to you."[16] It was correspondence such as this that linked him with her and the family he loved. On one occasion, while away, he wrote to her, "I cannot tell what a pleasure it would give me if I could have only one hour of your company. Here I am amongst many strangers and friends, but there is none that can fill that part of my heart that belongs to you."[17]

Campbell is often pictured, even by his friends, as a cold, aloof individual, guided primarily by his intellect. Some have stated that he took the heart out of religion and of human life. Louis Cochran, who wrote *The Fool of God,* countered this view by saying, "Nothing could be further from the truth."[18]

Campbell was a dedicated follower of Jesus. He believed strongly in worship, both in the assembly and in one's closet. He wrote that the worship of the Lord's Day should be "a display of the most rational and religious arrangement—a model, indeed, of the utility and beauty of the perfect order."[19] Admittedly, his argumentation does sound dry and cold. Campbell has been accused of that. However, one remembers that he lived at a time of great revivals, with huge camp meetings going on across America. Often they were wildly emotional, and Campbell was never really sure what to believe about them. He confessed that he was attracted by the powerful preaching, but was turned off by the uninformed fanaticism. Once, he stated that at these camp meetings, many taking place in the backwoods of Kentucky, likely "more people are conceived than saved."

Campbell felt that the only true revival came from God. He wrote that many revivals of his day were "a real disadvantage to the cause of true and vital religion."[20] Because of such excesses in religion, he

thought that the Christian cause was losing a great deal more than it was gaining. Conversion, Campbell said, is not something spooky or mysterious. Even during his early years back in Northern Ireland, he had sought God's Spirit through intensive study. He immersed himself in all the biblical passages on the Spirit, and read the contemporary evangelical authors. He even believed for awhile that he should

> look for a divine interposition of a peculiar character at a certain crisis and as the drowning man holds fast his straw, so we take hold of a dream, or a conceit, or an impression, or an impulse, or a voice, or a particular occurrence, and by a favorable interpretation imagine it a sign or token for good, and console ourselves that Heaven has now lent its long withheld aid.[21]

So, following his contemporary examples, he searched heaven for signs that he too was among the converted. Later he would come to believe that people sought this kind of experience because they had been taught to seek it and they had witnessed the testimony of others to it.[22] Instead, Campbell felt the Holy Spirit uses arguments addressed to the mind to bring sinners to right relationship with God. God was indeed active in converting sinners to Christ, but without any internal mysterious workings of the Holy Spirit.[23] In *The Christian System* Campbell wrote, "The Spirit of God inspired all the spiritual ideas in the New Testament, and confirmed them by miracles; and he is ever present with the word that he inspired."[24] A person simply needed to hear the facts of the gospel proclaimed, believe its testimony, and then through faith submit to immersion as evidence of the Spirit's authenticity.[25] Thus, one's confidence and eternal assurance rest upon the objective facts of the gospel. Statements such as these made many think Campbell was just too rational. J. Henshall, one of Campbell's early critics, believed that Campbell's views promoted "dry, formal, intellectual worship."[26]

Yet, there was another side of Campbell that needs to be seen, a side that evidences a warmer, more devout, and more pious person than usually noticed. Selena recalled that Campbell was by no means superstitious, yet he was a great believer in providence. It is she who told the details of Campbell's premonition while studying in Glasgow that God had great things planned for his life. She wrote:

> Alexander was alone in his study room, with his cloak on, and just on the eve of leaving to attend to his classes in college. Suddenly, and without any one being with her to introduce her, a very small, dark-visaged woman entered his room. His first impression was that she was a mendicant, and he put his hand into his pocket to get a shilling for her, in order to hurry her off. But she would not accept it, and before he was aware of it, she was calling attention to her writing on the mantle front before him, the names of his father, and mother, with his brothers and sisters; then, turning to him, she showed that she had no tongue, then turning each side of her head, no ears were there, only a small spot showing where the ears should be. She made him understand that he was going to a foreign country, and would be shipwrecked, but would escape, and blew up her apron like sails. Then, by unmistakable signs she made him understand that he was to preach to large audiences. She lifted her hand showing him how he would dismiss the multitude; all of which he fully understood by her emphatic gestures illustrating the meaning of her communication. Finally, she gave him to understand that he would be twice married, and left him without a doubt as to the full meaning of all her wonderful predictions which she persistently portrayed to him. Then as suddenly disappeared.[27]

On one occasion, Selena heard her husband remark that "nothing of importance ever happened to him without some indication or premonition being given to him."[28]

Body Language

Campbell believed that the Christian's face and conduct should always correspond to the Christian's heart. If the Christian's heart were pure, warm, and full of devout affections, then the outward person should display it. Body language, Campbell believed, was an important part of worship. Physical posture in prayer was vital. He said in 1835:

> To sit down and address God, as is very common at most family tables, in their thanksgivings for God's daily bounties, is most indecorous and disorderly. This, unless in cases of great physical debility, is not to glorify God with our bodies. Shall a man arise to address a respectable friend, and sit down to thank God for his daily repasts!. . . To stand erect, and lift holy hands—or to bow the knee before the Lord Almighty—or to prostrate oneself upon the earth, the footstool of Divine Mercy, is sanctioned by the examples of the great and wise, and good of all dispensations. (He mentions Solomon who fell to his knees before God; Jesus who fell on his face or stood and lifted eyes to heaven).[29]

He thought that the custom of his time of sitting for prayer came from a degenerate, apostate age, and was not known to earlier believers.

He returned to the topic again in 1845: "When you pray in church, kneeling should be preferred, when it could be made convenient. If not convenient, then standing was the required posture."[30] He viewed sitting as a posture of indolence. The correct posture of singing, especially with regard to hymns of praise, was standing. Indeed, it is considered more rational and scriptural than sitting. He viewed kneeling as a sign of submission, standing as a sign of reverence, and sitting as a sign of nothing. This was his view in 1845.

Thirteen years later, in 1858, Campbell wrote that he recently traveled through Iowa and Illinois and was shocked to find whole congregations sitting in the act of prayer. He wondered if they were skeptics or unbelievers. In his *Millennial Harbinger*, he reflected that a person does not sit down to address a king or an emperor. Furthermore, "sitting worshippers are lazy-bodies." He wrote wryly, "There are no sofas in the heavens for the aristocracies of the skies."[31]

Church members should always be punctual for assembly time. Campbell felt that being on time could be encouraged even more by the careful placement of the church entrance doors. There should be two exterior doors, and both should be placed on either side of the pulpit![32] Furthermore, one should not lavishly spend church finances in producing magnificent houses of worship. At the same time, he criticized those who let church buildings fall into disrepair.[33]

Campbell was not reticent to express his views on how the building itself should be arranged as best conducive for worship. He wrote:

> Pulpits are extremely absurd. The speaker ought always to be the lowest man in a house for three reasons; that he may have the best air, for he needs it most; that he may be easily seen; and that he may be distinctly heard . . . . This arrangement pre-supposes always that the floor be an inclined plane, of one foot in every eight, or, at most, ten, of its whole length. The ceiling ought never to be very high. It not inclined to suit the floor, it ought not to be more than twelve to sixteen feet high. No galleries, of course: windows large, and made to ascend and descend, that the room may be ventilated above or below, as circumstances may require. [34]

Campbell believed that the Christian assembly should be a solemn time, yet not too solemn. There is a place, he wrote, for "serious cheerfulness."[35]

Sing from the Heart

Campbell loved to sing, even though he could not sing well. He gave highest esteem to the Psalms of David, and commented that these "are my standard in all points of good taste, good sense, fervor, feeling, profound devotion, divine sentiment and every other element of pious wonder, love and praise."[36] He contended that many Christians were careless as they sang words of hymns, some of which even contained false doctrines.[37]

In 1828, he published his own hymnal, *Psalms, Hymns and Spiritual Songs*. His aim was to create a hymnbook suitable for family worship. From his youth, he had been shaped by singing in family worship. His new hymnal was adopted by many congregations, but his chief aim was for families to use it in their devotionals.

It is interesting that in all of his editions of his hymnbook during his lifetime, none contained musical notes. Campbell viewed notes as a distraction to the worshipper.[38] A worshipper needed to concentrate on the lyrics, and not be distracted by trying to perform. He stated his views more clearly in 1847: "I would prefer to have an organ, or a fashionable choir as a means of my worship rather than the words of a hymn set to the notes of a tune on which to fix my eyes while in the worship of God. Christians should not go to church to learn to sing."[39]

The following are the lyrics that Campbell wrote in one of his more famous hymns:

> Upon the Banks of Jordan stood—the great reformer John;
> And pointed to the Lamb of God—the long, expected One.
>
> Chorus: I see the blood of the Lamb; now I see the blood of the Lamb;
> 'Tis the blood of the Jesus the crucified; Now I see the blood of the Lamb.

Campbell took a conservative stance on dancing. He knew that the King James translation had the words, "Is any merry, let him sing psalms."[40] The writer did not say, "Let him dance." At the same time, if Campbell saw a Christian man or woman singing psalms and dancing, he would not condemn the individual. He was too good a student of the Word to overlook that David, in the Old Testament, was so full of joy on one occasion that he entered the temple walking and leaping while praising God. He knew that Jesus had also commanded his disciples to "leap for joy." Nevertheless, as in any age, there are some dances which are spiritually destructive, and Campbell encouraged parents to teach their children to avoid them.[41]

Family Devotions

Campbell was very much in favor of family devotionals. He had experienced them as a boy in his own family. Consequently, he recommended them for every household, stating in 1832: "How perfect are Christians who can dispense with the confession of any faults, who need never pray to God in secret, nor more than once a week or once-a-day in their families! Not so perfect was Paul and the first converts! They and he needed to pray always. . . . perhaps did we know, we might think it fitting to go and do likewise."[42]

One of the families that Campbell admired greatly was the Carltons. Olympas (father) and Julia (mother) Carlton had nine children (natural and adopted). Yet in their busy schedules, they found time to meet with the rest of the family twice a day for family devotions and readings. Campbell often passed through their home and witnessed their family worship style. As Campbell described it in the *Millennial Harbinger*, he said that it was more like family teaching, with both morning and evening lessons. The first "lesson" was from 6 to 7 a.m. He was so impressed with this method that he recorded about twenty pages of their conversation during the devotional in his 1849 journal. The family would read a passage of Scripture daily. All in the family would take turns reciting it. Next, the father would question each of the children on what they had read. Often these would be deep questions about the life or background of the apostle Paul. Campbell said that Olympas Carlton would also ask questions of the visitors in their home.

There were no passive spectators. After Campbell finished his report of the Carlton devotional, he respectfully recommended this "specimen" (of family devotion) to all Christian parents.[43]

Family worship, in Campbell's estimation, was of utmost importance. He wrote that the very first dispensation of religion was family worship. Indeed, there were families before there were tribes, nations, or churches. He told his readers that Christian families cannot hope to really rear their children well if they seldom or never gather them around their knees and allow them to hear prayers. He encouraged all heads of households in the church to make their families "*bethels*" (Hebrew for "house of God"), "to gather them around the Bible, morning and evening, to hear God speak to them through Prophets and Apostles, and their parents speak for them to God." Only in this way could families really permeate their minds with the fear and love of God.[44]

According to Campbell's plan, whole households should gather around the family Bible and paternal hearth, and hear the living word of the living God. Then, after oral instruction from a Christian parent, male or female, and a hymn of thanksgiving, all should fall down upon their knees before the Lord, and "from hallowed lips of kind and pious parent ascend to heaven prayers, supplications, intercessions for them all, in language appropriate, importune and devotional." He commented that surely the destiny of such a family will be different than a family that does not practice this.[45]

Campbell's personalized plan for his own family was to gather everyone, guests included, into the dining room for worship both morning and evening. Scriptures and hymns would be recited, followed by encouraging remarks from Campbell himself. He would then ask questions of those present on matters pertaining to the texts of the day. Robert Richardson in his *Memoirs of Alexander Campbell* described some of the scene:

> These being briefly considered, he would call upon Mrs. Campbell, who had a good voice, to lead in singing a psalm

> or spiritual song, in which he himself would heartily join, and then kneeling down would most reverently and earnestly present before the throne of grace their united thanksgivings and petitions for divine guardianship and guidance.... Family worship was not allowed to become a mere routine. He knew well how to maintain its interest, by making it a means of real instruction and enjoyment; and, by, encouraging familiar inquiry on the part of the young, he managed to bring forward and to impress indelibly the most charming practical lessons from the sacred writings, having always something novel and agreeable to impart zest and interest to exercises which in many cases are apt to become monotonous by frequent repetition.[46]

When preaching tours or other matters took him away from home, his wife, Selena, would take the lead in these faith-building services.[47] In one of his letters to Selena, while away, he encouraged her to continue with the family's spiritual training:

> I trust you are all attention, my dear, to your health, and, next to your health, the education and improvement of our dear children. Remember, this is the great business of life: to transmit to those, and through those to whom you have given birth, the knowledge of God and of his Anointed for their sakes and for the good of others yet unborn. In this way alone you can pay your debts.[48]

Later, after Alexander's passing, Selena reminisced about those times of family devotions:

> Nothing was permitted to interrupt the regularity of this sublime privilege. It was not attended to as a cold, formal duty, but it was made inspiring to all in attendance, by wife and children taking part, either in reading verses, turn about, in

> the precious book, or reciting passages of Scripture. Hymns were often recited, and sometimes chapters and parts of chapters. Servants were all called to be present; singing with spirit and understanding, accompanied by the family devotional exercises.[49]

As an indication of the whole family's dedication to the exercise, when Campbell left for a brief trip to Great Britain, Selena proposed to Wickliffe "the committing of the book of Proverbs in his father's absence."[50]

Pray More than Words

Campbell viewed prayer as communion with God. For those who might not be sure of what that means or think that it is too spiritual for earth, Campbell compared it to communion with another person, where one shares common sentiment and feeling. He wrote that it is "two sentimental spirits in conversation with each other . . . pouring into each other the overflowing of congenial views, feelings, and desires." Moreover, this communion involves conversation. God speaks to us through the Bible, his written word. Campbell declared that if one listens to God when he speaks, God promises to listen to the words of the prayer giver.[51]

Additionally, prayer is a special conversation. It is in prayer that one utters "our adorations, confessions, thanksgivings, petitions, and our unconditional submission to the will, authority, wisdom and goodness, mercy and love of him 'who is, and was, and evermore shall be!'"[52] He wrote that a Christian praying without the use of the means to obtain the object desired is ineffectual. Furthermore, the use of the means without the accompaniment of prayer is equally unsuccessful.[53]

Sometimes prayer is more than just the words one chooses to use. In his *Tracts for the People – PRAYER*, Campbell said that prayer is more than speaking to God and more than recognizing the existence of God.

Prayer also implies knowing about God, his attributes, and his omnipresence. It means knowing that wherever one is, God is. Furthermore, a Christian knows that God really does hear our voice, whether "vehement, impassioned and loud appeal" or "almost inaudible, whisper of a contrite, fainting, dying heart." Campbell shared that God can read what man cannot, i.e. those "groanings, those in-articulated aspirations and desires." The Lord is powerful enough to hear the "language of our agonies and unutterable sighs and emotions."[54]

In 1855, Alexander Campbell wrote that he was looking through a "long-neglected shelf of his library," and found a coverless volume of *Devout Meditations* by Edward Young, printed in 1754. As he flipped through the pages, he discovered that this old book had been given to him as a "premium for reading" when he was a child. It was at a period, he said, "beyond my earliest recollection of my school-boy days." In this book he believed he had found a real gold mine. He said that treasures such as these ought not to be lost. Here are a few lines concerning prayer from Campbell's rediscovered old volume (penned a hundred years earlier) which shared his temperament: "Prayer, unaccompanied with a fervent love of God, is like a lamp unlighted; and the words of one without love being as unprofitable as the oil and cotton of the other without flame."[55]

Private Devotional Life

Some of the most beautiful thoughts on prayer came when Alexander Campbell discussed private prayer. He wrote that the best school "under heaven" to learn prayer is really not in a class, but in one's closet, in fields, and in forests "where no human ear can hear us, no human eye can see us." It is there that one can practice prayer to one's heart content. These secret prayers are the prayers that influence the Christian the most. It is in those times where one really feels himself or herself in the company of God alone.[56] If asked when should a Christian do this, Campbell would answer that Christians must have stated "seasons of prayers," just like they have stated meals in their schedules. To best prepare for the encounter with God, one must have seasons of preparation to really enjoy and benefit from one's devotional time. He wrote, "We cannot profitably and reverently rush into the presence of God, as the horse rushes into battle."

One should have a time of self-examination. The disciple of Christ should enter the closet, shut the door, and then "converse with ourselves and with God by abstracting ourselves from the world in all its forms, cares, pursuits and pleasures."[57] According to Campbell,

> Prayer is naturally divided into secret and public, or into individual and social. The Savior commanded both. He gave promises to both—to him that enters into his closet, and to him who agrees with others touching anything for which they should unite in their prayers to God. Now in regard to secret prayers, there is less temptation to depart from the true and proper attitudes of prayer, than in public prayers: for in secret we are forced from any restraints or inducements growing out of a regard for the opinions and estimations of others.[58]

In one's secret prayers to the Father, which Campbell referred to as "heaven-devised appointments," a person expresses his wants and desires simply. He allows God to hear his real views and feelings. Indeed, one tells the Lord what one cannot tell any mortal, even the nearest and dearest on earth. As one prays, he allows God to hear all the heartaches, sorrows, and faults, as one pours out one's very soul with thanksgivings.[59] Campbell wrote: "There is everything in reason, in religion, and in our condition and circumstances, to entice us to the closet, and to allure us into the secret recesses to converse with our Father who is in heaven."[60]

Campbell believed that another person could usually tell when someone has not been engaging in private prayer. He wrote that when these people are called upon to pray in church, their language is "barren" and their style is "dry, frigid, and stiff." He argued that when one meets a person who prayed that way, he encounters a person who is "a great stranger to secret prayer."[61] Therefore, another good reason to pray in private is that it can help one to be less embarrassed when called upon to pray in public. Campbell believed that, "if we are long in conversing 'with the King,' we will never want language nor feel embarrassed when speaking in the presence of the King's servants."[62]

One of Alexander Campbell's favorite passages on private prayer was by Samuel Taylor Coleridge. Campbell admired the lines so much that he quoted them in the *Millennial Harbinger.*

> An hour of solitude passed in sincere and earnest prayer,
> or the conflict with and the conquest over a single passion
> or "subtle bosom sin," will teach us more of thought,
> will more effectively awaken the faculty, and form the habit of reflection,
> than a year's study in the school without them.
> A reflecting mind is not a flower that grows wild,
> or comes up of its own accord.
>
> The difficulty is, indeed, greater than many,
> who mistake quick recollection for thought,
> are disposed to admit;
> but how much less than it would be,
> had we not been born and bred in a Christian and Protestant land,
> very few of us are sufficiently aware.
> Truly may we, and thankfully ought we to exclaim with the Psalmist:
> "*the entrance of thy word giveth light; giveth understanding to the simple.*"[63]

Yet, in these private, secret devotions, Campbell encouraged more than prayer alone. Conversation with God should also include

> Meditation, self-examination, or what is called communing with the heart, communing with oneself, accompanied with the reading and study of the Word is the way, and the only way, to discover our wants, and the way to supply them; and to create those desires which will cause our spirits to breathe toward the skies and to pour themselves out in prayer and praise to God.[64]

The following words appeared in the *Millennial Harbinger* in December of 1853. The article had no name attached to it, and so it is not known whether these were Campbell's own words or not. Yet, Campbell, as editor, approved of these thoughts, and preserved them for all to consider.

> If a preferred disciple would not have his business become a millstone around his neck, to drown him in perdition, he must be a man of prayer; he must daily secure spiritual communion with God. If he suffer his business to consume his time and spirits so as to deprive him of opportunities for prayer, reading the Bible and real communion with God, he must decay in piety, and his service of mammon eat up his service of God. No one who believes that God answers prayer will think of omitting either secret or family devotion for want of time, even when business is unusually urgent. Which is worth most to you or your family, additional period of your own un-blest labor, or the blessing of God on your efforts, obtained by spending that time in pleading with him in prayer? The plea of want of time, is essentially a-theistical; none should urge it but those who regard prayer as an empty mockery, that never receives an answer from the Lord. Let the day begin with communion with God; let the disciple pass the whole day in the spirit of prayer, and all its duties will become spiritual duties, and all its scenes be inscribed with "Holiness to the Lord."[65]

Such thinking and practice, if brought again to twenty-first-century churches, could go a long way to alter individual as well as corporate character and reputation.

In conclusion, Alexander Campbell did, in fact, have a more spiritual and heart-felt side than is usually recognized. One might even posit that he called upon his brain's "right hemisphere" often to better himself and others. People frequently sought him out because of his personable style and ease at religious conversation. Perhaps because his inner devotion was more secret than publicly displayed or flaunted, insiders within the Stone-Campbell movement have missed the encounter with the complete man. Selena, his second wife, knew more than anyone the true warmth of his character. She wrote lovingly, "He was always happy, cheerful; ever uncomplaining, unmurmuring, and never fault finding, always ready to find something to praise and approve of—whether at home or abroad. Such was the tenor of his noble life! Indeed how could he be otherwise than happy—love was the supreme topic with him—love to 'God supremely, and love and good will to men!' I do believe no happier man ever lived."[66]

Unmistakably, Campbell could write well from his head, and preached with supreme logic and rational thought. Perhaps, however, such empowerment came from those quieter moments of the heart spent alone with the Master of all.

Chapter One Notes

1. Arlie Groover, *The Well-Ordered Home: Alexander Campbell and the Family* (Springfield: Hastings Press, 1967), 14.
2. Ibid., 18.
3. Ibid., 19.
4. Ibid., 20.
5. Ibid., 22.
6. Quoted in Thomas H. Olbricht, "The Holy Spirit in the Early Restoration Movement," *Stone Campbell Journal* 7:1 (2004): 111, 112.
7. Ibid., 27.
8. Alexander had begun the habit of rising at 4 a.m., even as a youth. This habit continued throughout his adult years. His second wife, Selena, wrote that to enable him to get his lessons when he rose so early, he kept a bowl of water beside his bed in which to plunge his face. Selena Campbell, *Home Life and Reminisces of Alexander Campbell, by his wife Selena Huntington Campbell* (St. Louis: J. Burns, 1882), 289.
9. Groover, *Well-Ordered Home*, 22.
10. Ibid., 32.
11. Ibid., 34.
12. Sparks asserts that Campbell's wealth came through his journals, but, more often than not, the publications barely broke into the black financially. Elder John Sparks, *Raccoon John Smith: Frontier Kentucky's Most Famous Preacher* (Lexington, Ky.: University of Kentucky Press, 2005).
13. Antebellum America saw a great rise in the number of debating societies. They became widely popular, and functioned not only as institutions of education, but also as entertainment and mass communication. Alexis de Tocqueville reported that Americans were so attracted to these "clubs," that they often took the place of theaters. Alexis de Tocqueville, *Democracy in America*, trans. George Lawrence, ed. J. P. Mayer (1966 reprint, New York: Harper Perennial, 1988), 243.
14. Selena Campbell, *Home Life,* 340.
15. Most of these are now available online at Hans Rollman's webpage. http://www.mun.ca/rels/restmov/people/acampbell.html
16. Loretta Young Honeycutt, *The Life of Selena Campbell: A Fellow Soldier in the Cause of Restoration* (Tuscaloosa, Ala.: University of Alabama Press, 2001), 53. Campbell often referred to Selena as his "fellow soldier" because of her equal participation in his work. See "Letter to Selena" (March 12, 1839).
17. Alexander to Selena, October 12, 1829.
18. Louis Cochran, "The Private Life of Alexander Campbell," speech given at the Disciples of Christ Historical Society, 1962.
19. Alexander Campbell, "The Order of the Church as Respects Worship," *Millennial Harbinger* 6 (October, 1835): 508.
20. Campbell, *Millennial Harbinger* 2nd series, no. 4 (April, 1840): 167-8.
21. Campbell, "Reply to the Above," *Christian Baptist* 4 (June, 1827): 228.

22. John Mark Hicks, "God's Sensible Pledge": Witness of the Spirit in the Early Baptismal Theology of Alexander Campbell," *Stone Campbell Journal* 1 (Spring, 1998): 10.

23. Max Ward Randall, *The Great Awakenings and the Restoration Movement* (Joplin Mo.: College Press, 1983), 360. Campbell, *The Christian System*, 48.

24. Ibid. In essence, conversion is always the work of the Word and the Spirit. Campbell explained his conviction about the Spirit more clearly in his debate with the Presbyterian Rice. "I believe the Spirit accompanies the Word, is always present with the Word, and actually and personally works through it upon the moral nature of man, but not without it. I presume not to speculate upon the nature of this power, nor the mode of operation. I believe the Holy Spirit sheds abroad in our hearts the love of God, and dwells in all the faithful; that it sanctifies them through the truth; that 'it works in them to will and do,' and that it comforts them in all their affections." *A Debate Between Rev. A. Campbell and Rev. N.L. Rice on Christian Baptism* (Lexington, Ky.: A. T. Skillman & Sons, 1844), 745.

25. Hicks, "God's Sensible Pledge," 19.

26. J. Henshall, "A Hint to the Disciples," *Millennial Harbinger* 5 (January, 1834): 34. He further warned that this "reform is too likely to consist in eradicating the feelings altogether."

27. Selena Campbell, *Home Life*, 292.

28. Ibid., 293.

29. Campbell, *Millennial Harbinger* 6 (1835): 488-489.

30. Campbell, "Church Organization," *Millennial Harbinger* 3rd series, no. 2 (February, 1845): 66.

31. Campbell, *Millennial Harbinger* 5th series, no. 1 (1858): 37.

32. R. Edwin Groover, "The 'General Apostasy from Good Taste and Good Sense': Alexander Campbell's Critique of Fashionable Religion," *Stone Campbell Journal* 2 (Spring, 1999): 10.

33. Ibid., 12.

34. Campbell, "Incidents on a Tour to the South—No. II," *Millennial Harbinger* 2nd series, no. 3 (February, 1839): 56

35. This *serious cheerfulness*, according to Campbell, should be "equi-distant from the morose austerity of Pharisaic sanctity and the thoughtless gaiety of Sadduccean levity." Campbell, "Order," *Millennial Harbinger* 6 (October, 1835): 508. Groover acknowledges that "serious cheerfulness" is an oxymoron, saying that it walks a tightrope which undoubtedly required more self-control than emotional spontaneity—which smacked of ostentatious display. Groover, "The General Apostasy," 15.

36. Campbell, "Psalmody," *Millennial Harbinger* 2nd series, no. 7 (March, 1843): 129.

37. Groover, "General Apostasy,"18.

38. Campbell, "The Christian Psalmist. Proposals," *Millennial Harbinger* 3rd series, no. 4 (March, 1847): 179. Other Christian groups at the time were also not using musical notations in their hymnals.

39. Ibid.

40. James 5:13.

41. Selena Campbell, *Home Life*, 430. Baptists, Methodists, and Presbyterians all opposed dancing, believing that, like other amusements, it distracted people from seeking religion. Barton Stone also spoke publicly against it. D. Newell Williams, *Barton Stone: A Spiritual Biography* (St. Louis: Chalice Press, 2000), 38.

42. Campbell, *Millennial Harbinger* 3 (1832): 64.

43. Campbell, *Millennial Harbinger* 3rd series, no. 6 (1849): 2-23.

44. Ibid., 10.

45. Ibid., 11.

46. Robert Richardson, *Memoirs of Alexander Campbell, embracing a view of the origin, progress and principles of the religious reformation which he advocated* (Cincinnati: Standard Publishing, 1913), 2:300-301.

47. Honeycutt, *The Life of Selena*, 8.

48. Letter to Selena (June 11, 1836).

49. Selena Campbell, *Home Life*, 19.

50. Ibid., 32, 36. She recalled that Campbell had one time said that every child ought to commit to memory the book of Proverbs.

51. Campbell, *Millennial Harbinger* 3 (1832): 123.

52. Ibid., 124.

53. Ibid., 126.

54. Ibid. (1849), 3.

55. Ibid. (1855), 612.

56. Ibid. (1832), 498.

57. Ibid. (1849), 7.

58. Ibid. (1832), 498.

59. Ibid., 499.

60. Ibid.

61. Ibid.

62. Campbell realized his theory had an exception. He said that a person cannot be fluent in prayer if he were not fluent in speech on other subjects. In this case habitual secret prayer would not help. Ibid.

63. Samuel Taylor Coleridge, quoted by Campbell in *Millennial Harbinger* 4th series, no. 1 (1851): 540.

64. Campbell, *Millennial Harbinger* 5 (1834): 292.

65. Ibid. (1853), 701.

66. Selena Campbell, *Home Life,* 315.

Chapter Two

BARTON W. STONE

Seeker of the Polar Star

PART ONE: Barton's Story (1772-1844)

The Early Years

Barton Warren Stone was born in Charles County, Maryland, on the eve of Christmas, 1772. John Stone, his father, had married Mary Warren Musgrave and was a well-to-do Maryland planter. The Stone family line went back to the founding of Maryland. Among the earliest of Maryland governors in the 1640s had been Captain William Stone. As reward for his service to the state, he received 5,000 acres along the Potomac. The Stones of the 1770s were faithful members of the Church of England and baptized young Barton as an infant. His father died when Barton was three years old. The first seven years of his life were spent in Maryland until his mother decided to move the family into the Dan River Valley, deep into the Virginia frontier, Pittsylvania County, near the North Carolina line. However, father Stone had not left the family destitute, willing them a considerable amount of money which mother Stone used for young Barton's first education in Virginia.

That first teacher, Stone recalled, was a "tyrant" who seemed to take pleasure in whipping and abusing his students for the least of offenses.[1]

In his autobiography, Barton Stone remembered at the age of nine watching while his older brothers left home to fight in the Revolutionary War. He wrote that he would never forget the sorrows of his widowed mother when her sons shouldered their firearms and marched away to join the army.[2] The Stones lived a mere thirty miles from the fields where General Green and Lord Cornwallis met in combat, and young Barton often winced from the blasts of noisy artillery rounds.

As a boy, Barton had a strong desire for books. Printed material was hard to procure, so Barton was able to read only a few, but the ones he read, he read over and over. Two of his favorites were the Bible and a secular novel, *Tom Jones*. The latter was not the best of help for the development of life skills, but his early reading inaugurated his lifelong thirst for knowledge. He stated that he took "great delight in books, and preferred them to any company, and often retired from my young companions to indulge in the pleasure of reading."[3] Those early years revealed the inner, deeper side of Stone as well: "For some time I had been in the habit of retiring in secret, morning and evening, for prayer, with an earnest desire for religion; but being ignorant of what I ought to do, I became discouraged, and quit praying, and engaged in the youthful sports of the day."[4] Stone's father's estate was finally divided among the siblings, and Barton decided to invest his inheritance in his education at the David Caldwell Academy in North Carolina. His plan and heart's desire was to be a lawyer and a statesman, thus continuing the Stone family lineage.

On February 4, 1790, Barton entered what was nicknamed the "Log College." Indeed, the entire campus consisted of a two-story log cabin with a few cabins scattered around it as dormitories. The average yearly enrollment was only thirty to fifty students.[5] Caldwell Academy was also a seminary for training Presbyterian ministers and commonly entertained visiting ministers who occasionally held revivals there. Among all the classical academies in the region, Caldwell had the best reputation.[6]

Conversion to Christ

Soon after entering the academy, Barton noticed that some of the students had been influenced by James McGready, a popular preacher known both for his piety and engaging style. Barton also witnessed these pious students assemble every morning in a private room before the hour of recitation to sing and pray. To him they appeared sincerely devoted and happy. Barton wrote that at this time he felt guilty and uneasy sharing the campus with them. He believed it was better not to think about it. Getting involved with religion would slow his academic progress. Yet his conscience bothered him, so much so that he could neither "enjoy the company of the pious nor the impious."[7]

On one occasion David Caldwell heard the Calvinist James McGready preach, and invited him to visit his school. Caldwell was a New Light Presbyterian. This group believed that religion was something that had to involve the senses, and not just belief in the right facts and living morally.[8] McGready was one who could stir the senses and was already known far and wide as a great revival preacher. He had a wild and emotional style. His sermons smoked the chairs with the fires of hell. If success was measured in the number of visible converts following a revival, McGready's revival at Caldwell was thoroughly successful. Almost the whole student body was converted. The lone holdout was Barton Stone. Technically, Stone was still an Episcopalian. Following the revival of McGready at the Academy, Stone said that he was made to feel his sin but not hope. Moreover, he could not ignore the new converts. They devoutly assembled every morning early to sing and pray in a private room. Witnessing their sincere piety only made him notice his own lack thereof.[9]

McGready returned to campus on other occasions. Once when Stone heard McGready speak about the wrath to come, Stone commented, "Such was my excitement, that had I been standing, I should have probably sunk to the floor under the impression." As the meeting closed, Barton returned to his room. He wrote, "Night coming on, I walked out into an old field, and seriously reasoned with myself on the all-important subject of religion. What shall I do?"[10] But again the answer was not revealed. Stone said of McGready, "He left me without one encouraging word." If he really believed that McGready was speaking truth, he knew his own plans would have to change. To this his heart said, "No." At the same time, he did not want to go to hell either. For a year Stone's inner struggle continued.[11] In fact, this struggle did not surprise him. From his previous exposure to Baptists and Methodists in Pittsylvania County, he had come to expect a "long and painful struggle" before he would be "willing" to "come to Christ."[12] He prayed, hopeful, then uncertain; seeking, then ceasing, nearly despairing of ever getting the hope of the eternity he desired.[13] By Calvinistic doctrine, there was always the possibility that he was among those who might never be saved.

Then, another preacher, William Hodge, visited the academy with a different approach. Whereas McGready's sermons had stressed judgment, Hodge stressed the love of God. Stone said that he had heard so many preachers "thundering divine anathemas" that Hodge's idea of the love of God appeared as some new doctrine. So after hearing that God is love, Barton declared, "I immediately retired to the woods alone with my Bible. Here I read and prayed with various feelings, between hope and fear." Stone came to love this "new" God. Moreover, according to Presbyterians, to find one's heart "warmed" with the love of God and to find something "new" in the preaching of what God had done for sinners were signs of conversion.[14] In fact, Stone wrote, "(I) adored Him—I praised him aloud in the silent night in the echoing grove around."[15] Barton Stone was converted, and became interested in the Presbyterian ministry. From that event on, until he finished his course of study, he devoted his life to God, even finding pleasure, as he said, in the "study of dead languages."[16]

But a Presbyterian needed a license to preach. In those times, the process involved preaching a trial sermon before the Orange Presbytery, the ruling body in Western North Carolina. Stone's topic, the Trinity, was pre-assigned, and was a difficult topic even for well-seasoned preachers. Barton's friends helped him put it together. He preached the sermon and the Presbytery accepted it. The process for licensure would then be completed in six more months, but the biggest hurdle had been achieved. Yet Stone never received the license. He withdrew from school instead. He said he had too many misgivings about Calvinism which lay, he believed, at the heart of Presbyterianism. He also had depleted his education funds.

Stone thus broke off his study of theology and headed further south. His older brother lived in Washington, Georgia and could perhaps assist him in finding employment. Shortly Barton got a job teaching in new private school[17] run by Hope Hull, a Methodist minister. Stone took the job as a teacher of languages.

Methodists, on the whole, were less inclined to Calvinism, but they were fervently devout, and this rekindled Stone's desire to preach. He had also been constantly attending the preaching of John Springer, whom Stone described as a "very zealous Presbyterian." It was under Springer's preaching that Stone "began to feel a very strong desire again to preach the Gospel."[18] As a result, Stone returned to North Carolina in 1796 and received his preaching license. However, he backed away again, thinking the task was too solemn. So, with his license to preach hidden inside his baggage, he slipped away to a place where no one would know him. But hiding in a "distant country" did not last long. A pious elderly woman there discerned who he was and accused him of imitating the reluctant prophet Jonah. She advised him to set out for the West where the Lord would surely find use for him.[19]

Go West, Young Preacher

Many people at the time were migrating to Kentucky with its beautiful wilderness. Stone joined them. As he traveled, he relied on people's hospitality. Along the way, he went through Nashville, which he described as a "poor little village scarcely worth notice."[20] It was during his migration to the West that Stone began his journal. He kept it among his most valued possessions and forty-seven years later when he penned his autobiographical sketch, it enabled him to graphically narrate this earlier period. He recalled on one occasion relying on the hospitality of a fellow Christian, but having his sleep interrupted by pests of the night. He included his comments in Latin, afraid that a gracious host might read it and be offended at his ungracious statement of fact. When translated, the English reads, "At night fleas disturb me, and they drive away sleep. I am weary of life."[21]

Upon reaching Kentucky, he decided to settle in Lexington, at the time the biggest city in America west of the mountains. There were already some friends there from Caldwell. In Lexington, he began preaching for two small Presbyterian churches nearby, one at Concord and the other at Cane Ridge. The latter's region had been so named by Daniel Boone for the wild cane that grew there.[22] For two years (1796-1798), Stone brought the Christian message to these backwoods residents.

These Kentuckians loved Stone and pushed him to become an ordained pastor, not just one with a license only. However, to obtain ordination he must agree with the Presbyterian creed, the famous Westminster Confession. Ordination would then be decided at the formal meeting of the Presbytery of Transylvania. Stone was thankful for their love and their zeal for him, yet there remained one lingering problem. All along he had had trouble with certain tenets of Calvinism. He thought that perhaps if he studied the Bible more, he might be able to accept these teachings. However, the more he studied, the more he stumbled at the doctrines of predestination, election, and even the doctrine of the Trinity. Expressing his agitation over the Presbyterian Confession he wrote:

> Often when I was addressing the listening multitudes on the doctrine of total depravity, their inability to believe—and of

> the necessity of the physical power of God to produce faith; and then persuading the helpless to repent and believe the gospel, my zeal in a moment would be chilled at the contradiction.[23]

In other words, he did not even believe his own preaching. The struggle was intense. He said, "Sweat profusely burst forth from the pores of my body and the fires of Hell gat [sic] hold on me."[24] In the months of waiting for the ordination ceremony, he tried to avoid these doctrines and just preach sermons on practical living. In fact, facing the question he knew was coming, he had carefully planned his answer. It would be an answer to the question asked of all candidates: "Do you accept the Westminster Confession of Faith?"

The time arrived and the crowd was assembled. He responded loudly, so all could Hear: "I do, as far as I see it consistent with the Word of God."[25] As an answer, it was certainly not typical, but the committee agreed it was sufficient.

Barton Stone was thus ordained, but his heart remained full of uncertainty. For the next couple of years Stone struggled with his friends, struggled with the text, and perhaps even more disheartening, he struggled with apathetic, lazy congregations.

The Frontier Family and Cane Ridge

The Cane Ridge meeting was the zenith of Stone's life. He wrote about it in great detail in his autobiography. By contrast, he devoted only one line to his wife, Elizabeth. He said, "My companion was pious and much engaged in religion." According to local custom, his neighbors "lifted" a log cabin for him, and it was here that he brought his new bride straight from her father's house. Elizabeth blessed Barton's life for nine years. She died, leaving him with one son and four daughters.[26] Later, the son would also die. Life on the frontier was rough. Stone remarried and had six more children. At the time of his own death, he would have a total of forty-nine grandchildren. John Rogers, a long-time friend and biographer, and who had been in the Stone home many times, praised Stone's commitment to family:

> He carefully brought up his children in the nurture and admonition of the Lord; night and morning asking the divine blessing upon his family, and committing and commending himself and them to the care and protection of the Heavenly Father. His was truly a house of prayer—his a Joshua's resolution: "As for me and my house, we will serve the Lord."[27]

Stone was twenty-eight years old when the revival came to Kentucky. Historians analyze it as part of the Second Great Awakening that had swept the East and was now coming West. Following the Revolutionary War, churches were demoralized and the nation as a whole became extremely apathetic towards spiritual concerns. Less than ten percent of the country held membership in any church.[28] The part of Kentucky not far from Stone's home had numerous reports of lawlessness, and had been nicknamed "Rogues Harbor."[29] Peter Cartwright, the Methodist circuit rider, wrote of the area:

> Here many refugees, from all parts of the union fled to escape punishment or justice. For although there was law, it could not be executed and it was a desperate state of society. Murderers, horse thieves, highway robbers, and counterfeiters fled there until they combined and actually formed a majority.[30]

Churches were declining in central Kentucky. Methodists, who kept the best records of any frontier denominations, recorded a drop of sixty-seven in their Kentucky membership for the years 1792-1800; and this was the time in which the population of the whole state nearly doubled.[31]

This drought of spirituality was ready for a flood. In this new western phase of the awakening, it moved into regions with excitement. The revival moved quickly past the limits of New England and the intellectuals. The young nation was moving west, and many of those who went west took with them their new-found gospel. But in the West, conditions were different. The setting was much more emotional, and noticeably less intellectual. Around the year 1799 the atmosphere changed dramatically. In that year a Presbyterian pastoral letter stated that, although there was still much immorality and vice, "we have heard from different parts the glad tidings of the outpourings of the spirit, and of times of refreshing from the presence of the Lord. . . . From the east, from the west, and from the south, have these joyful tidings reached our ears."[32] Even greater joy and expectation was expressed in 1801:

> Revivals, of a more or less general nature, have taken place in many parts, and multitudes have been added to the church. . . . From the west, the Assembly has received intelligence of the most interesting nature. On the borders of Kentucky and Tennessee, the influences of the Spirit of God seem to have been manifested in a very extraordinary manner.[33]

Things were developing quickly. In 1796, the evangelist James McGready had taken this kind of preaching to the West. Like Stone, he too had moved to Kentucky and became pastor of three small churches—Muddy River, Red River, and Gasper River in Logan County. McGready was always a fearless preacher, and he informed his hearers that "they had not left the eternal God behind them." He proclaimed that "God was as much on the frontier as he was anywhere." McGready spoke in angelic terms of heaven and its glories, thundered about hell and its torments, and questioned his hearers about their salvation. His message was so powerful that by 1798 many were "struck with an awful sense of their lost estate."

By June 1800 these revivals attracted attention all across the state. Stone had to investigate for himself. Perhaps he could even learn something to take back to his own lethargic congregation. Stone knew that those who were snoring needed to be awakened, but it must be done with the right message. So in curiosity as well as anticipation, Stone traveled to Logan County to observe McGready's work. He returned to his own work, believing this present revival really was "the work of God." He wrote, "Many old and young, even little children professed religion, and all declared the same simple gospel of Jesus. I knew the voice and felt the power."[34] To Stone, the voice was the voice of God, and the power was the power of the gospel.

He returned home and soon planned similar meetings for Concord and Cane Ridge. The first of the two was held on the first Sunday of June, 1800. It was a sacramental service that would climax with the sharing of the Lord's Supper. It was also the largest religious meeting in the state of Kentucky to date. Stone's estimates were between five and six thousand in attendance.[35]

Stone was busy. Approximately a month before the Cane Ridge meeting, he married Elizabeth Campbell.[36] Yet, the plans for the next sacramental service continued. It was held in August, 1801. It was better publicized than Concord, and the numbers that arrived, coming from as far as Ohio and Tennessee, were estimated between 10,000 and 25,000. This number is remarkable in that Kentucky's recorded total state population was only 220,095 in 1800.[37] The meeting began on Friday, August 8, and continued through the following Wednesday. The Presbyterians had sent invitations even to Methodist and Baptist preachers from far and near, and Stone was delighted that all appeared to work in unison. He wrote, "They were of one mind and soul: the salvation of sinners was the one object. We all engaged in singing the same songs, all united in prayer, all preached the same things."[38] One contemporary described the Cane Ridge camp meeting, in an account that could represent similar meetings of that period:

> The careless fall down, cry out, tremble, and not infrequently are affected with convulsive twitching. . . . Nothing that imagination can paint, can make a stronger impression upon the

> mind, than one of those scenes. Sinners dropping down on every hand, shrieking, groaning, crying for mercy, convulsed; professors praying, agonizing, fainting, falling down in distress, for sinners or in raptures of joy![39]

Another observed there were people "crying for mercy; some shouting redeeming grace; and others collected in numberless small circles of twelve or twenty singing hymns; all serious; many walking to and fro, with anxiety pictured on their countenances."[40] Added to this were several ministers preaching at once! One participant described the cacophony as that of Niagara Falls.[41] Cane Ridge became famous not only for its numbers, but also for its excesses of enthusiasm. Visitors witnessed or participated in hysterical laughter, trances, falling and shaking (as if succumbing to grand mal seizures), and occasionally even more bizarre forms of behavior.[42] This wildness was of course grossly exaggerated and enemies often used accounts of them to discredit the camp meetings. Some skeptics declared, "More people were conceived than saved at these meetings." Nonetheless, none could deny that audiences at these frontier awakenings did become highly emotional. People

moved from wagon to wagon to hear the various thundering sermons. What had been the peculiar differences of doctrines between the groups began to break down. There was a common appeal to all persons to come to Christ. The clear message was that all had a chance at salvation, not just the elect. The excitement was contagious and the meeting would have continued for a longer time had it not been for the scarcity of food.

While Stone was never personally affected to any perceptible degree by these "bodily exercises," his attitude was that of sympathy and pragmatism.[43] If in the end people were brought to Christ, perhaps these activities could be used.[44] Presbyterian synods, however, were far less charitable. Soon the synods began condemning any minister who had taken part in such meetings. Stone himself was condemned as a heretic.

Just "Christians"

Stone concluded it was the time to join with other like-minded ministers, break from the Presbyterian Church, and form the Springfield Presbytery (1803). He was also commissioned to write a defense of their action. He labeled it, "An Apology for Renouncing the Jurisdiction of the Synod of Kentucky." Within just a year, however, this same group issued their "Last Will and Testament," believing that Scripture did not authorize their existence. Instead, they decided to just be Christians. He wrote, "We dissolve ourselves into the Body of Christ at large. . . ."[45] For the rest of his life, Stone was convinced that "Christian" was the name followers of Christ should wear.

Stone was certainly a child of the revivals and their influence. Yet, he was also deeply committed to Scripture. As an example, after breaking from the Presbyterian Synod of Kentucky, he went before his own congregation to announce that he could no longer conscientiously preach to support the Presbyterian church. He let the congregation know that they were no longer under any obligation to support him. In a visual demonstration, he ripped up their contract with him before their eyes. Such honesty, perhaps more for himself than for his congregation, caused him to sacrifice an abundant salary. Stone believed that he was now dependent only on the Word of God and it would carry him through.[46] Truth and an inner peace was preferable to any friendships or associations in the Presbyterian ministry. So without support from congregations and having just freed his slaves, he wrote that he turned his "attention cheerfully, though awkwardly, to labor on my little farm. Though fatigued in body, my mind was happy and calm as summer evenings be."[47] In fact, by the summer of 1804, Stone thought that the millennium might just be dawning. Christians were liberating their slaves. The Spirit was at work in uniting Christians, and new light was shining from God's Word.[48]

Such a stance of volunteer church labor was radical for his time. Frontier life was already hard enough, and with the loss of professional income and slaves the situation at home turned strenuous for the whole Stone family. He returned home to work the farm by himself, and to preach without pay, nearly as often as before. On several occasions, he would return home from his preaching circuits and find the weeds outgrowing the corn. He would then stay out in the field until late at night.

Stone's early years apart from the Presbyterian Synod were not easy ones, and some of his closest associates returned to the Presbyterian Church. Others joined the Shakers, a new religious group on the Kentucky frontier. Barton wrote to a dear friend, Richard McNemar, "O my Richard, shall I ever rejoice over you as a penitent prodigal."[49] In later years, Stone thought back about this discouraging time and bemoaned, "Of all the 5 of us that left the Presbyterians, I only was left, and they sought my life."

"Like Fire in Dry Stubble"

However, something was happening. Before 1804 had ended, fifteen churches had sided with Stone and his ideas. Seven were in Ohio and eight in Kentucky. By 1807, there were twenty-four churches in four states. These became part of a great reforming movement that swept across Kentucky and Middle Tennessee like "fire in dry stubble." Then in 1832, this movement joined forces with Alexander Campbell's group based in upper Virginia. Stone moved to Illinois and preached there for several years. He continued to preach until the 1840s when he began to have a series of strokes that left him paralyzed and deaf.

Stone's message was that Christian unity was vital and should be based upon the Bible. He also initiated a new journal, *The Christian Messenger* (1826). Many of his articles encouraged unity among Christians. Estimates are that by 1832 (when Stone's group united with Campbell's), the Stone group had nearly ten thousand members in Kentucky alone.

PART TWO: Barton's Heart

The Polar Star

Barton Stone led a great unity movement. He felt that unity was his polar star, guiding and directing all of his messages and actions. Stone stated that there are four kinds of union. First, there is "Book Union" based on a creed. Second, there is "Head Union" founded on opinion. Third, there is "Water Union" based on immersion. Fourth, there is "Fire Union" founded on the spirit of truth. To be sure, Stone had witnessed all of the above four as he mingled among the churches of several states. He felt, however, that only the fourth union was worthy of one's energy and cooperation. He was convinced that this was the type of union for which Jesus prayed. Stone judged all human attempts at union as vain. He wrote that it would be like tying bundles of twigs together and hoping they would somehow bear fruit. These individual branches must first be united to the living stock, and receive its sap and Spirit before they can ever be united to each other. One must, therefore, be united with Christ and receive his Spirit prior to any hope of being united with each other. [50]

Life in the Spirit

According to Stone, the Bible is clear in its teaching that the entire work of regeneration and salvation from sin emanates from the work of God's Spirit.[51] He stated in an 1836 article that he was aware of many who boasted about having the Spirit, but were destitute of it. Stone asked, "Have they the spirit of grace and supplication? Do they pray in secret, and with their families night and morning? If not, is not their religion vain? Is it better than moral infidels?" He wrote that all Christians have the Spirit. He quoted Paul in Romans 8, "If any man have not the Spirit of Christ, he is none of his." At the same time, he felt that not every Christian is full of the Spirit. He mentioned the seven individuals in Acts who were chosen because they were "full of the Spirit." Paul exhorted Christians to be filled with the Spirit (Eph. 3:16; 1:17). Thus, any Christian can properly pray for the Spirit to be given in greater measure.[52] To be sure, part of one's devotional life is a recognition that the Holy Spirit must be involved.[53]

When compared to Alexander Campbell, Stone spoke a great deal more about the Spirit. He even left open the possibility that the spiritual gifts of the first century might be around in his time. A Christian cannot exist without the Bible, God's Word, but neither can one exist without the Spirit of God. He declared, "Some appear to make the Scriptures everything in regeneration; and others make them nothing." Both these opinions he considered as extremes. He gave this example:

> Suppose God should extend his arm from heaven, and hand the Bible to me a poor sinner, and thus address me: 'Take this book—in it are all things necessary for you to know, believe

and do—by this book, convert, regenerate, quicken, and save yourself; never expect any other help, aid or assistance from me.

On this plan I should think it folly and presumption to pray to God for his spirit, or for anything—I should despair of salvation and eternal life.

Again; suppose God should hand me, a poor sinner, the Bible, and should thus speak:

"Take this book—in it are all things necessary for you to know, believe and do—but you can neither know, believe nor do them, till I, in my sovereign time and way, give my Holy Spirit, to enlighten and renew your minds."

On this plan I should think it folly to attempt to know, believe or do. To act consistently would be to lie inactive, and wait for that sovereign time, if that time should ever come.

That which I think to be the truth, is this: Suppose God, having handed me the Bible, should thus speak: "Take this book—in it are all things necessary for you to know, believe and do—believe them as the truths of Heaven, and come to me and ask, and I will give you the Holy Spirit, and every promise of the New Testament." On this plan I should be encouraged to activity in every duty, in the confident expectation of help and salvation.[54]

A few decades later, Robert Richardson published similar thoughts in the *Millennial Harbinger*. He felt that those who promoted the "Word only" held to a view that was "cold and lifeless" and only estranges from God.[55] Richardson was concerned that in the latter part of the nineteenth century the current reformation avoid the extremes of both spiritualism and rationalism—as he preferred to describe them, "Spirit only" and "Word only." The "Word only" extreme was just as unscriptural and spiritually fatal as the "Spirit only" extreme.[56]

During the 1830s and 40s, Stone became distressed over some (especially from Campbell's side) who felt that the gifts of the Spirit had ceased with the age of the apostles.[57] In 1844, Stone said in reply to one who commented that Stone's movement lacked organization, "The great secret of church government and organization has almost been overlooked. It is the indwelling of the Holy Spirit in each believer and member of the church."[58] Stone advised preachers to preach "in the Spirit," yet he observed the Spirit was not to be confused with a "great vociferous zeal and manner" which might be "nothing more than mere animal nature."[59]

Those who knew Stone knew him as a great man of God, and a man of the Spirit. Nearly everyone detected a spiritual quality to his leadership. One biographer penned, "In his personal life, he paramounted (sic) the Spirit."[60]

Loving Humility

Barton Stone was not just a man of the Spirit. He was also known for his kind, loving, and humble heart. John Rogers, one of the earliest biographers of Stone and himself a preacher in the Stone-Campbell movement, said this about him:

> [His] entire life has been made up of tenderness, amiability and love. As a husband he was fond, indulgent, kind. As a father, he was mild, affectionate, impartial. As a brother, faithful; as a friend, ardent and unwavering. . . . The cause of his Savior was nearest his heart, in youth, manhood, and old age. Christianity was his theme in life—his comfort in death.[61]

Rogers also wrote of Stone's almost universal respect. He was even loved by many who were opposed to his religious ideas. Rogers knew that there were many who criticized Stone's doctrine, but none could criticize his character.[62]

One time Stone wrote to his friend James Blythe, urging him to realize, "The best doctrines in the Bible unless they form the heart and life of humility, gentleness, and love, will never give an entrance into heaven."[63] Stone was convinced that a Christian's heart must be touched by the message. If not, then the message is just cold doctrine. One writer contemporary to Stone praised his "gentle, meek and quiet spirit" and said that "the law of love was on his tongue."[64]

For decades Stone's name was known to thousands of Christians. One wonders how Stone himself must have felt about being placed in leadership position of a great movement. A lesser man would have given in to the temptation to be less than humble. John Rogers reflected that few men can "bear prosperity and popularity, so as to retain the humble spirit of religion."[65] Yet Stone never gave it any thought. He seems to have been continually unconscious of his place in the movement. In his modesty, he would have preferred the lowest seat at a gathering. One writer commented, "Though he stood at the head of a great reformation-movement in the West, yet he never seemed to realize that such was his position, and he abhorred the idea of being a leader of a party."[66]

This trait of humility was noticeably prominent in his words, actions, and numerous writings. In the introduction to both editions of his Address, he wrote: "Believing mankind to be fallible creatures, we therefore feel a spirit of toleration and union for all those Christians, who maintain the divinity of the Bible, and walk humbly in all the commandments and ordinances of the Lord Jesus Christ, and who live by faith in his name, though they may hold opinions contrary to ours."[67] He believed that outsiders should also exercise that same spirit toward Stone's group. Indeed, if such occurred, he felt, all could be mutually edified and the cause of the kingdom could advance, and surely the "foul blot on Christianity, the division of Christians, might be wiped away, and thus a powerful weapon against revelation be wrested from the hand of infidelity."[68]

In one of his lectures on Matthew's Gospel, Stone expounded the verse "Blessed are the poor in spirit" and said that the phrase meant humility.[69] This type of person must be convinced of his own natural poverty of things divine, such as holiness, righteousness, and peace. James Mathes, who co-edited the *Works of Elder B. W. Stone*, felt that Stone's sense of natural poverty led him to pray more.[70]

Stone also wanted to protect his expanding movement from false pride. He wrote: "Whenever we rejoice in the increase of our number more than in their reformation from sin, and their increase in holiness and piety, we ought immediately to take the conviction of being wrong, and not rest till, by the grace of God, the evil be corrected."[71]

Dependent Prayer

In his later years, Stone wrote several articles addressed to young preachers. He told them: "Be holy out of the pulpit as in it. . . . Be often on your knees, always endeavor to keep God before your mind, and labor to please him, rather than man."[72]

One time someone asked the question, "If God knows all our needs, why do we need to pray?" Stone responded by saying that this kind of question was really an insidious as well as sophisticated objection to prayer. Prayer must produce in us a spirit of dependence and gratitude. He compared prayer to the earthly parent who is rich with every blessing, including many children. The parent would be happy if the children enjoyed all these great things. At the same time, the godly parent must teach each child dependence and "excite in them the divine virtue of gratitude. The Lord of heaven has ordained therefore, that his earthly children ask him for what they need."[73]

Stone loved to be around congregations that prayed. It was always encouraging to be with others who believed in worship and in the power of prayer. In 1832, Stone was asked why more people do not really participate in true devotional worship when they are together. Stone responded, "[In singing] we find them everywhere actively engaged, but in praying and exhorting one another, they are everywhere deficient." In too many places Stone witnessed congregations that neither "prayed nor exhorted" until the preacher arrived.[74] The blame for this, he said, was on Christian teachers. They have neglected this important teaching and have not urged congregations to pray. Another reason was simply that members neither knew their duty nor obeyed it.[75]

Stone was not reluctant to criticize congregations with lackluster worship services. He noticed that, in many places, when the preachers ascended the pulpit they delivered one long discourse after another until the congregation became "wearied and fatigued." Such exhaustion was clear in the fact that as soon as the doors opened to let the congregation escape, "each flies to his hat—puts it on in the house of God, and makes a rush to the door, like children being dismissed from the disagreeable toil of learning in a school room."[76] Stone was convinced that congregations where members were regularly well fed on heavenly food, and their minds engaged and impressed with the solemnity of truth, would linger inside church doors much longer.[77]

One of the reasons Barton Stone moved to Illinois was to escape the evils of American slavery in the lower states. In his own family he owned some servants who were tied to his children. By his leaving the state of Kentucky, he knew they could be free. Yet, physical distance would not separate his heart from them. In 1838, he returned to Kentucky. He had missed his former servants living now in Georgetown. Rogers wrote that this Kentucky homecoming was like that of a father visiting his children. Stone visited with them a long while, encouraging them. He asked about their temporal and spiritual welfare. Then, before he left he proposed that they pray. "All present bowed down before God, while his tremulous voice and feeling heart went up to God in devout supplication. Tears flowed from all eyes. The parting scene was truly affecting."[78]

Stone's view of one's physical posture in prayer was similar to Campbell's. Both leaders insisted that one's bodily position was just as important as what was being expressed in the prayer itself. Most of the early Stone-Campbell leaders shared these feelings. Stone thought that Christians should pray on their knees, if at all possible. He wrote in the 1843 *Christian Messenger*:

> Another thing which I have seen and deplored, which is too common everywhere...the indecent mode of the congregation's worship in prayer. Some were kneeling, others sitting, and others standing in time of prayer. Now there may be cases in which a congregation cannot kneel, as in a great crowd; but few cases can justify the posture of sitting. It does not show reverence. Many appear afraid of sullying their fine garments by kneeling. This pretext should be removed by having the floors of the houses clean. . . . There is hardly a more serious sight on earth, than to see a congregation kneeling in prayer before their God.[79]

Value of the Quiet, Inner Person

Stone never made any pretense to being a poet. Nevertheless, he has left a few pieces that evidence again his quieter, inner heart. One such piece was the eulogy that he composed on the death of Elizabeth, his wife. The poem was more than twenty verses long. A few of the lines read:

> If Prophets did such victories swell,
> A greater victory, I'll tell
> Gained o'er the powers of death and hell,
> E'en by a feeble woman.
>
> Death's cruel art prepared a dart,
> Which pierced Eliza's peaceful heart;
> and twelve revolving months the smart
> Had stripped her blooming vigor.
> Her soul in patience she possessed,
> Still panting for the promised rest;

And tho' with helpless weakness pressed,
Yet shouted praise to Jesus.[80]

Another Stone composition beautifully visualizes a weeping willow tree that hung over the grave of Elizabeth and their infant son.

Beneath this grassy turf lies innocence and love;
The willow bends its flexile boughs above;
Nor is her son, deep-sleeping by her side,
Forgotten by the mourner, far-spread wide;
It waves its boughs o'er his infantile head,
And sweeps the tomb, and murmurs o'er the dead.[81]

Stone proposed that the face the preacher revealed to his congregation on Sunday should be the same face any day of the week. He believed strongly that every Christian (and especially ministers) really allow the Christ to live in one's inner self. He affirmed, "A preacher should never preach a doctrine to the people, the power and efficacy of which, in converting and building up into Jesus, he has not experienced, does not experience in himself. Then truly is he eloquent, and earnestly speaks what he knows to be true, not only from the testimony of the Word, but also from a heartfelt experience of its power, leading him to Divine love and obedience."[82]

While Campbell had grown to appreciate the use of debates, Stone rejected this practice as a way to spread the faith. He wrote, "debates tend to strife, deaden piety—destroy the spirit of prayer –puff up the vain mind . . . and destroy the comforts of true, heavenly religion."[83] Thomas Miller Allen, a long-time friend, later eulogized Stone:

I doubt whether there ever was a purer, better man than Elder B. W. Stone. His entire life was little else than a practical commentary on the pure faith and morality of the gospel he professed. While many have denounced him for heresy all, I

> believe, concede the fact, that the meekness of his temper, the quietness of his spirit, his humility were those of a Christian.[84]

Stone placed high value on the interior of a human being. He believed that external attempts at displaying spirituality were sometimes silly. He wrote:

> Outward ornaments, and costly apparel, with a servile imitation of the fashionables of Europe, however whimsical and extravagant, have fearfully absorbed the almost entire attention of our females, and kept their parents and husbands in perfect drudgery to support them. But little time can be devoted to the improvement of the mind, to the practice of religion.[85]

Stone related that during one of his meetings, the house and the passage were literally packed with people. Suddenly, two ladies entered wearing large hooped sleeves. Stone said the sleeves looked about four feet across. They were also wearing sparkling jewelry from their ears and other extravagant jewelry. Stone wrote that he noticed quickly,

> the extreme difficulty they had to encounter in passing through the crowd toward the pulpit—they had to walk sideways; and when they were seated, it was found that, though there was room sufficient for three of their size, yet they could not sit in less than two feet of each other without annoying each other, and spoiling their hooped sleeves. The consequence was, that one or the other had to stand up during the time of worship. I pitied their folly; but abhorred their taste.[86]

Stone felt that these women should have spent less time and money on the superficial externals and focused more on their inner selves.

On rare occasions, however, Stone's own quiet interior could become quite public. In his later years, Barton grew increasingly deaf. He attended one church service, and spoke to the preacher in private,

"You know I am deaf—speak loud—I want to hear every word." The theme of the sermon that morning was justification by faith, taken from Romans 5. The preacher became somewhat excited in his preaching, reaching one of those high point climaxes. Suddenly the elder Stone yelled out from the audience, "Glory be to God!" This sudden disruption thoroughly rattled the preacher. Stone observed the man's confusion and embarrassment, so he yelled smilingly, "Go on, brother; go on!"[87]

Stone also treasured song as a way to encourage and enhance one's spiritual devotion. Yet the lyrics as well as the tunes must be chosen carefully. He wrote in his *Christian Messenger* in 1843, "True, they sing, but too often with new theatrical, or piano tunes applied to sacred songs without solemnity either in the tune or the singer—only a few join, the rest being unacquainted with the tune or the song, and before it is learned, another of the same class is introduced."[88] He offered his own selections by writing several hymns for his own hymnal, as well as assisting in the production of Campbell's *Psalms, Hymns and Spiritual Songs*.

Last Advice

Not long before his death, Barton Stone wrote an article that never made its way to any journal. It was discovered after his death among his personal notes and papers. It was addressed to fellow leaders in the ministry. In this essay, Stone wrote that he noticed a spirit of strife springing up among public Christian teachers, and especially journal editors. He feared that great evil would result from such a spirit. His personal ambition had always been to promote peace and good will among Christians. He recommended the good, though rare advice of an elder to one of his preaching brothers, "Be humble,—be humble, —be humble."[89]

One of Stone's published articles contained a fictional interview between an elderly minister and a young one. The old preacher obviously stood for Stone himself and his current feeling about the brotherhood. In the interview the old preacher warned the younger, pointing out some trouble spots that might lie in the road ahead. He commented: "Another cause [for concern] is the great want of piety and devotion to God and his cause, in the professed ministers of the Gospel. Without these we can never hope for better days." Younger preachers, Stone believed, should obviously know doctrines and how to defend them. Sadly, however, he knew people who arrogantly defend their doctrines, and tell each other never to yield on one point or submit to one argument, however "just and plain." Moreover, there is an over abundance of pride in the ranks. Stone continued:

> The hours set apart for meditation and secret prayer are neglected, or, if attended to, are interrupted, and the thoughts of the heart are diverted to these divisive doctrines, how they can be established or overthrown to advantage. When the Scriptures are read, it is not to hold converse with God—to learn duty and do it—but to find something there to establish their received doctrines of controversy. When the pulpit is ascended, the burden of the sermon is the agitated controversies of the day, teaching the congregation the art of war. The same subject is continued in private circles.[90]

In 1844, the year of his death, Stone complained in a final series of articles that many in the movement placed biblical knowledge, religious controversy, and debate above "godliness, piety and brotherly love." He asked: "Do we see genuine Christianity promoted by such controversies and debates? Look around and enquire for these fruits. Do you know of any person spiritually renewed or refreshed with spiritual understanding? Do you find brotherly love and Christian union advanced? On the contrary, do you not find their opposites promoted?"[91] John Rogers related that, as Stone neared his end, he reminded his family again about the importance of family devotions and prayer.

> He called his family around him, and admonished them individually, as he had been accustomed when in health, to fill the various relations they occupied, with honor to themselves and to God. He told his bosom companion, "not to grieve, but to go home and show the world, how a Christian mother could bear such a heavy loss." He told her "never to forget family prayer," and further said to her, "tell my brethren their religion is of no avail, unless it leads them to the family altar."[92]

In one of his final letters, Stone wrote from his current home in Illinois back to his beloved church at Cane Ridge. He told the members that he never forgot Cane Ridge and the memories of the great times there. He finally reflected: "My prayer is that whenever we may be called from earth, we may joyfully answer the call. May we all—old and young—black and white, meet in our Father's house above, and be forever with the Lord."[93]

Chapter Two Notes

1. D. Newell Williams, *Barton Stone: A Spiritual Biography* (St. Louis: Chalice Press, 2000), 11.
2. Hoke S. Dickinson, *Barton Stone, The Cane Ridge Reader* (Paris, Ky.: Cane Ridge Preservation Project, 1972), 2.
3. Ibid., 4.

4. Ibid., 5.

5. Not a bad number, considering the time and place.

6. Williams, *Barton Stone*, 17.

7. Dickinson, *Cane Ridge Reader*, 7.

8. D. Newell Williams, "Barton Stone in 1804: From Port Tobacco to Cane Ridge," *Stone Campbell Journal* 7.2 (Fall, 2004): 191.

9. Ibid.

10. Dickinson, *Cane Ridge Reader*, 8.

11. Olbricht reflects that many of the sermons of the itinerant preachers in the Second Great Awakening chiefly focused on the need for long, personal struggles in order to receive the Holy Spirit and be assured of one's salvation. Thomas H. Olbricht, "The Holy Spirit in the Early Restoration Movement," *Stone Campbell Journal* 7.1 (Spring, 2004): 7.

12. Williams, *Barton Stone*, 23.

13. Dickinson, *Cane Ridge Reader*, 9. Presbyterians, Baptists, and Methodists of that era assumed that the awakened sinner's period of seeking conversion prior to receiving it, which they aptly referred to as "distress," would typically last from several weeks to a year. Williams, *Barton Stone*, 197.

14. Williams, *Barton Stone*, 27.

15. Dickinson, *Cane Ridge Reader*, 11.

16. Ibid.

17. There were no public schools at this time.

18. Williams, *Barton Stone*, 34.

19. Dickinson, *Cane Ridge Reader*, 17.

20. Nashville's population at the time was roughly three hundred.

21. Charles Crossfield Ware, *Barton Warren Stone, Pathfinder of Christian Unity: A Story of His Life and Times* (St. Louis, Mo.: Bethany Press, 1932), 57; Dickinson, *Cane Ridge Reader*, 18.

22 . There are also legends of Indians who would hide out in the cane in warfare.

23. Dickinson, *Cane Ridge Reader*, 31.

24. Ware, *Pathfinder of Christian Unity*, 82.

25. Dickinson, *Cane Ridge Reader*, 30.

26. Williams, *Barton Stone*, 132. Williams wonders if a factor in the cause of Elizabeth's early death might have been the bearing of five children within eight years before age twenty-six.

27. Quoted in Dickinson, *Cane Ridge Reader*. Rogers also says of Stone, "In patience he possessed his soul. He had learned in the school of Christ the invaluable art of self-government." Dickinson, 248f.

28. Bill Humble, *The Story of the Restoration* (Austin, Tex.: Firm Foundation Publishing House, 1969), 4. The exact number of church attendees was probably higher since part of the reception process into formal church membership was the appearance before the church elders or leaders and relating a conversion experience.

29. Williams, *Barton Stone*, 49.

30. Peter Cartwright, *Autobiography of Peter Cartwright* (Bibliolife Reproduction Series, nd), 4.

31. Williams, *Barton Stone*, 51.

32. Extract from "Report of the General Assembly of the Presbyterian Church of the United States of America" (1799).

33. Extract from Report of General Assembly (1801).

34. Dickinson, *Cane Ridge Reader*, 35.

35. Williams, *Barton Stone*, 56.

36. No relation to Alexander or Thomas.

37. Williams, *Barton Stone*, 59.

38. Dickinson, *Cane Ridge Reader*, 69.

39. Extract 26. "Of a letter from the Rev. Moses Hoge, of Shepherds Town, to the Rev. Ashbel Green, of this city, dated Sept. 10, 1801."

40. Ibid.

41. Williams, *Barton Stone*, 61.

42. See Stone's autobiography for further details of the "bodily exercises." See also Hans Rollman's website: http://www.mun.ca/rels/restmov/texts/bstone/barton.html#ch_six

43. Stone was always much more sympathetic than Campbell to these emotional activities displayed in the revivals.

44. This is Ware's analysis of Stone's reluctance to condemn them. Ware, *Pathfinder of Christian Unity*, 113.

45. Both documents are available on Hans Rollman's website: http://www.mun.ca/rels/restmov/texts/jburnett/opc/OPC.HTM#Will

46. Dickinson, *Cane Ridge Reader*, 297.

47. Ibid.

48. Williams, "Barton Stone in 1804," 209.

49. Ware, *Pathfinder of Christian Unity*, 169.

50. Ibid., 258.

51. Barton Stone and James M. Mathes, *Works of Elder B. W. Stone*, 141.

52. *Christian Messenger* 10 (1836): 20.

53. Stone felt, however, that unlike the Father and Son, the Spirit could not be referred to as a person. He noted that in the Bible we "often read that the Father loves the Son, and that the Son loves the Father; but we never read of either the Father or the Son loving the Spirit as a person, or of the Spirit loving the Father or the Son." Further, he said, "We have neither example nor precept for worshipping the Spirit in the Bible." Stone, "Letters to Blythe," 25-29.

54. Mathes, *Works of Elder B.W. Stone*, 142f.

55. Robert Richardson, "Spirit of God—No. VII," *Millennial Harbinger* 2nd series, no. 7 (1843): 560-561.

56. Richardson's views are clearly spelled out in five series of articles for the *Millennial Harbinger* devoted primarily to the person and work of the Holy Spirit, as well as several other single articles, and especially his magnum opus on the Spirit, a 324 page book, entitled *A Scriptural View of the Office of the Holy Spirit*, (Cincinnati: Bosworth, Chase & Hall, 1873). See also Steve Singleton, "Robert Richardson on the Holy Spirit: Balance between Rationalism and Spiritualism," *Stone Campbell Journal* 1 (Fall, 1998): 155-166.

57. Richard Hughes, *Reviving the Ancient Faith: The Story of Churches of Christ in America* (1996; 2nd edition, Abilene, Tex.: Abilene Christian University Press), 100.

58. Ware, *Pathfinder of Christian Unity*, 330.

59. *Christian Messenger* 12 (August, 1842): 316-320.
60. Ware, *Pathfinder of Christian Unity*, 331.
61. Rogers' biography of Stone, quoted in Mathes, *Works of Elder B.W. Stone*, 34.
62. From Rogers in Dickinson, *Cane Ridge Reader*, 262.
63. Ware, *Pathfinder of Christian Unity*, 210.
64. From Rogers in Dickinson, *Cane Ridge Reader*, 250.
65. Quoted in Anthony L. Dunnavant and Richard Harrison, eds., *Explorations in the Stone-Campbell Traditions: Essays in Honor of Herman A. Norton* (Nashville: Disciples Divinity House at Vanderbilt University and Disciples of Christ Historical Society, 1995), 12.
66. Dickinson, *Cane Ridge Reader*, 300.
67. Ibid., 13; Stone, *An Address*, 2nd ed., 31.
68. Stone, *An Address*, 6-7; see also 2nd ed., 4.
69. *Christian Messenger* 12 (1841): 23.
70. Mathes, *Works of Elder B.W. Stone*, 223.
71. Ware, *Pathfinder of Christian Unity*, 330.
72. Mathes, *Works of Elder B.W. Stone*, 343.
73. *Christian Messenger* 7 (1833): 202.
74. Williams, *Barton Stone*, 246.
75. *Christian Messenger* 6 (1832): 280.
76. *Christian Messenger* 13 (1843): 132-33.
77. Ibid.
78. Letter to Rogers from A. Adams, in Dickinson, *Cane Ridge Reader*, 294.
79. *Christian Messenger* 13 (1843): 168.
80. Dickinson, *Cane Ridge Reader*, 311.
81. Ibid., 317.
82. Mathes, *Works of Elder B.W. Stone*, 210f.
83. Quoted in Hughes, *Reviving the Ancient Faith*, 105.
84. Ware, *Pathfinder of Christian Unity*, 332.
85. *Christian Messenger* 6 (1832): 242.
86. Ibid.
87. Dickinson, *Cane Ridge Reader*, 304.
88. Stone, *Christian Messenger* 13 (September 1843): 132-33.
89. Dickinson, *Cane Ridge Reader*, 279.
90. Mathes, *Works of Elder B.W. Stone*, 210f.
91. Quoted in Hughes, *Reviving the Ancient Faith*, 105.
92. From John Rogers, quoted in Mathes, *Works of Elder B.W. Stone*, 35.
93. Dickinson, *Cane Ridge Reader*, 284.

Chapter Three

WALTER SCOTT

Voice of the Golden Oracle

PART ONE: Walter's Story (1796-1861)

He has been called one of the "Big Four" of the Restoration Movement, along with Barton Stone and the two Campbells (Alexander and Thomas). At the front entrance to the Disciples of Christ Historical Society in Nashville, Tennessee, there stands a four-sided obelisk, with each side showing a face in relief. Walter Scott's likeness resides on one of the sides. Many agree that Scott's greatest contribution to the Stone-Campbell movement was as an evangelist, a preacher of the good news of Christ.

It was sometime during the winter of 1821 and 1822 when Alexander Campbell first met this young Scotsman. Campbell realized quickly what an asset to the cause Scott could be. In fact, it was Scott's personality and drive that led the Campbell group to separate from the Baptists. Walter Scott has been nicknamed the "Voice of the Golden Oracle." The "Golden Oracle" was Jesus the Christ, and Scott was his spokesperson. Above the door to his classroom every entering student saw that phrase in big chalk letters drawn there by Scott himself.

Early Training

Scott came from unpretentious beginnings. He was born on October 31, 1796, in Moffatt, Scotland. His parents had given birth to ten children, five sons and five daughters. Walter was the sixth child. His father, John Scott, was a celebrated music teacher, while his mother was deeply religious. Both of them wished their son to become a Presbyterian minister. Walter possessed a natural aptitude for music, studied the flute, and developed great musical ability. At one time he was said to be the most skillful performer in the whole city.

An early event in his life showed a side to young Walter that one does not view often in teenagers: compassion. He was sixteen years old, and while walking through the downtown streets during a busy holiday season, came across a beggar sitting by a bridge and holding out his hat for any passerby's spare change. Walter had nothing to give, but was thoroughly moved. Suddenly, an idea came into his head. He would stand there and sing by the beggar's side. A crowd soon collected, and when he finished the song, made an appeal for pennies. The grateful impromptu audience responded with a shower full of them. The older brother had been out searching for Walter, and was thoroughly surprised when he discovered him. He had always thought Walter was bashful, and here was shy Walter singing publicly long into the night. This heart of compassion, demonstrated at such a young age, would later lead Scott to have compassion for people's souls as well.

The times were financially difficult for the family. Luckily, the State Church of Scotland (Presbyterian) selected Walter to be educated and helped with his expenses. From 1812 to 1818, Scott attended the University of Edinburgh. Though not certain, historians assume that Walter Scott graduated from the university. This is because 1818 was the year when about ten to fifteen Walter Scotts graduated. Following this formal schooling, his uncle sent an invitation to Walter's parents to send one of their sons to America, assuring the family that he would continue to assist that son in advancing his career there. So in 1818 Walter immigrated to America, and as far as can be known, never returned to his homeland nor saw his parents again. Later in 1821, the tragic news came to America that both his parents had died at the same time. Reports were that Walter's father had gone to a neighboring village in Scotland and died very suddenly. When the information came to his mother the shock was so great that she collapsed and died immediately. Both were buried at the same time in the same grave.

Walter arrived in New York City on July 7, 1818, and spent a year there teaching Latin. The following year he heard the call to go west. There had been numerous glowing reports of a great region beyond the Allegheny Mountains. So, believing the reports, Scott migrated to western Pennsylvania in 1819, to the growing new city of Pittsburgh.

The "Kissin' Baptists"

In Pittsburgh, Walter met a fellow Scot, George Forrester, who was to change his life. Forrester was conducting an academy and also running a private high school for boys. He was also preaching for a church that had been influenced by the Haldane brothers and had broken with the Presbyterians. Back in Scotland the Haldanes had called for a return to the New Testament, and were attempting a restoration of beliefs and practices of the church of the first century. Forrester took them quite literally, and had begun practicing immersion, as well as the "holy kiss." People in the area nicknamed them the "Kissin' Baptists." However, they referred to themselves as the "Church of Christ." They also practiced washing of feet, not as a liturgical ritual, but as an act of brotherly kindness and Christian hospitality. Within just a short time, consequently, Scott was both teaching in the academy and associating himself with the Haldane congregation. He would spend many hours with Forrester in intensive Bible study. Like Forrester, Scott began to be impressed with the authority of scripture. Moreover, through his Greek study he became convinced that sprinkling and pouring were human substitutes for the style of baptism enjoined by the apostles. Walter Scott was soon immersed by George Forrester.

The joy of new beginnings did not last long. A crisis came in 1820 while Forrester was swimming in the Allegheny River. He drowned, leaving the church and the academy to the care of his gifted associate. Scott was devastated. With the death of Forrester, Scott was deprived of his dearest friend, and the small church of its beloved and faithful shepherd. Walter Scott became both the principal of the Academy and preacher for Forrester's church.

Walter Scott seemed captivated with the simplicity of the gospel. He would spend every spare minute studying the Bible, and was able to access Forrester's library. The library possessed an excellent collection of biblical commentaries, Benson's work on the Epistles, McKnight's *Harmony of the Gospels*, Catchbull's Notes, Haldanes' Works, Campbell on the Four Gospels, Locke's *Reasonableness of Christianity*, and so on.

While working in Pittsburgh in 1821, Scott came across a little tract on baptism published by a church in New York. It was entitled "On Baptism" by Henry Errett,[1] a member of a congregation of "Scotch Baptists." Among other things, the tract stated that baptism is for the remission of sins. This was a new idea for Scott. At the time, no one was preaching baptism for remission of sins. Scott was intrigued and thought he might learn more from paying the church a visit. Consequently, he closed the Academy, and went east to New York. The trip, however, turned into a dismal disappointment. The life of the church there failed to live up to what Scott thought was implied by the tract. He remained there only three months, realizing the declining church was spiritually dead. When Nathaniel Richardson wrote to him to return to Pittsburgh to serve as a tutor for teenagers, Walter eagerly accepted the offer. On his way back to Pittsburgh, Scott stopped at several East Coast cities. In Baltimore, he found a small congregation in very bad condition. There was also a body of worshippers in Washington, DC, but Scott found them sunk in the "mire of Calvinism, that they refused to reform; and so finding no pleasure in them I left them. I then went to the Capitol, and climbing up to the top of its lofty dome, I sat myself down, filled with sorrow at the miserable desolation of the Church of God."

Upon returning to Pittsburgh, Walter Scott lived in the Richardson home, where he would serve as a private tutor to Robert,[2] the man's son, and a few other young men. One afternoon Scott was out walking with Robert Richardson in a garden beside his school. Robert handed his tutor a rose. Scott took it, breathed in its fragrance, admiring its tints, and then posed the question, "Do you know why in the Scriptures Christ is called 'Rose of Sharon'?" Young Richardson admitted that did not know the answer. Scott responded that it is because that particular rose has no thorns. Jesus, like the rose, is utter, unblemished beauty.[3]

It was during the winter of 1822, while residing at the Richardson home, Scott first met Alexander Campbell, who was staying overnight and enjoying the hospitality of their mutual friend. They became close friends for forty years. Campbell was impressed with Scott's intellect and spiritual insights. He informed Scott, "Walter, I want to begin publishing a new paper, and I'm going to call it *The Christian*. What do you think?" Scott liked the idea of a paper, but suggested that Campbell use the name *Christian Baptist.* He knew that Campbell was laboring among the Baptists, and including their name in the title would probably encourage more Baptists to read it. During the next seven years, Scott contributed a number of articles to the *Christian Baptist* and signed all of them simply as "Philip." In his relationship to Campbell, he viewed Alexander as the new Martin Luther and himself as Philip Melanchthon, Luther's friend, the prophetic voice of the movement.

New Associations

In 1823, at the age of twenty-six, Walter Scott married Sarah Whitsette. The next ten years blessed them with six children. In 1826, they moved to Steubenville, Ohio, where the family resided for one year. The next year, they moved to Canfield, Ohio, where they would stay for four years.

Some of the churches in this part of Ohio had joined the Mahoning Association. First organized in 1820, the Association consisted of ten churches in northeast Ohio, which was called the "Connecticut Western Reserve," still part of the American frontier. In 1826, six other churches joined. In the early nineteenth century, one of the most prominent features of frontier American religion, especially on the Western Reserve, was revivalism. In 1827, the Association proposed that they send an evangelist to travel among them. These churches in the Mahoning Association were more receptive to Campbell's ideas. Indeed, several of them had thrown out creeds and resolved to follow only the Bible. But these churches were not growing. It was obvious that something was wrong. Campbell's reforms were practiced in the churches, but they were not gaining appreciably in numbers. Some were lukewarm, others cold or dying. Robert Richardson stated the problem: "There had indeed been an almost entire neglect of evangelization on the part of the few churches which were originally connected with Mr. Campbell, in his reformatory efforts. They had not a single itinerant preacher, and, although they made great progress in biblical knowledge, they gained comparatively few converts."[4] In 1827, the Association chose Scott as their evangelist, though he was not a Baptist nor a member of any of their churches. It was Campbell who suggested Scott. The Association unanimously went with the suggestion and Scott worked as their evangelist from 1827 to 1830.

The "Experiment"

In this new position, Scott knew he would have to give up his church, his academy, and even leave his family for awhile. He had also been planning a periodical, *The Millennial Herald*. A few years later, Scott wrote about being selected:

> I never made one objection to the nomination, nor to the appointment, but saw in it a providence, I believed no mortal then understood but myself. I immediately cut all other connections, abandoned my projected Editorship, dissolved my Academy, left my church, left my family, dropt the bitterest tears over my infant household that ever escaped from my eyes, and set out under the simple conduct of Jesus Christ to make an experiment of what is now styled the ancient Gospel.[5]

In actuality, it was an experiment. Walter Scott could study and teach, but could he preach? He himself was not really sure of how to go about it. As he began the "experiment," he focused on the question, "How does one preach the gospel as it was preached in the early church?" Scott decided upon the simple plan to just preach Jesus. He had concluded that the central point of the whole Christian faith and the core of the Bible is the truth that Jesus Christ is the Son of God, the Messiah. His view was that this newly discovered truth was a precious jewel to be treasured. He labeled it the "Golden Oracle."

Of Scott's early preaching, he wrote later that during his first sermons, "people fled." To many listeners, Scott came across as sincere, but deluded. His words would excite wonder, pity, and even scorn. Many people thought his sermons contained a new message, perhaps even an heretical one. The first real response came on November 18, 1927 in New Lisbon, Ohio at a Baptist church. That day Scott spoke at great length about Peter's confession of Jesus in Matthew 16. He then turned to Acts 2, Peter's proclamation. Four years earlier, he had preached a similar message, but had stopped at verse 37, "What shall we do?" However, this time Scott continued and preached with great force: "Repent and be baptized every one of you, in the name of Jesus Christ for the remission of sins, and you shall receive the gift of the Holy Spirit." There was one response, a prominent Presbyterian businessman, William Amend. Mr. Amend made his way through the crowd and asked to be baptized. In the years that followed, Scott would go on to help thousands more, so this first response stands with a certain historical significance. Later Scott wrote to Amend, asking about his response that day. Amend wrote back that he had been waiting for years for the right message. He said that if he ever heard anyone preach the gospel like Peter did on Pentecost, he would obey it. Amend searched the Scriptures himself and looked for years trying to find someone to baptize him. His own Presbyterian minister refused to do it. Finally, after many years of waiting, Walter Scott came to town. Amend had sat skeptically that day outside the building, An overflow crowd had spilled out into the yard. But Amend slowly made his way into the hall. In his letter to Scott he informed him that he only got to hear the last five minutes of the sermon. But it was enough. Amend sat down at the front, ready to be baptized. In his letter to Scott, he reminded Scott of the final points of that sermon: "The Scriptures no longer shall be a sealed book. God means what he says. Is there anyone present who will take God at His word, and be baptized for remission of sins?" Amend stated that when he heard that, he said to himself, "Glory to God! I have found the man whom I have long sought for."

A New Man and New Plan

While William Amend had found his man, Walter Scott had found his plan. He now believed that the original New Testament plan of salvation was being preached and recovered for the church of his day. Earlier, Alexander Campbell had restored the "Ancient Order." Scott believed it was just as necessary to restore the "Ancient Gospel," that is, Jesus as the true Messiah, and the correct steps in the process of salvation. Thus, the phrase "Gospel Restored" meant not just preaching and clarifying the plan of salvation, but also baptizing individuals for the remission of their sins, accompanied by the reception of the gift of the Holy Spirit.

This bold new move was not without its controversy. On one occasion, a woman had requested baptism. But her son said, "If Scott baptizes her, I'll shoot him!" Walter Scott wrote to Campbell, "In one place where I was baptizing, just as I raised the baptized person out of the water, I saw a great stick hanging or rather shaking over my head." On another occasion, he was interrupted by a person wielding a sword cane. At another place, they set Scott's horse, his means of transportation, loose in the night.[6] Despite the occasional, at times violent protests, Scott became a highly successful evangelist. There are some estimates that he baptized a thousand people per year for thirty years. One who heard him preach on the Western Reserve said of him: "Scott was different from James McGready and all of those preachers at the Cane Ridge revival. His message was a clear and simple one. . . . What I remember quite clearly is that he quoted a lot of scripture when he preached. Scott called on people to accept Jesus Christ as the Messiah and Son of God."[7] Scott's evangelism was unique in that it consisted of a simple rational and scriptural plan of salvation, calling for a personal relationship with Jesus Christ as Messiah and Son of God. To those with a background in Calvinism, who were experiencing doubts and uncertainties regarding the eternal destinies of their souls, Scott's message was strongly objective and straightforward.[8]

Thomas Campbell heard about these revivals occurring in the Western Reserve and went to investigate for himself. Thomas returned and told his son, Alexander, that Scott had finally found a practical way of applying what they both held in theory, but had not been able to effect. Thomas said, "We have had the right theory, but I am seeing it practiced for the first time." Even though it had been nearly fifteen years since the Campbells themselves were baptized by immersion, they had really baptized very few up to Scott's time. The intellectual Campbells were great on doctrine, but could not excite and move people. The fledgling movement needed a fiery and effective preacher like Scott.

Often he would go during the day to schoolhouses just as the children were getting out of school. He loved children, and usually a large circle of kids would gather around him. When the young crowd had assembled, Scott would say, "Now, children hold up your left hand." They all did so, mimicking Scott's movement, some wondering what game this old fellow was about to play with them. He would then say, "Now, beginning with your thumb repeat what I say to you—Faith, repentance, baptism, remission of sins, gift of the Holy Spirit—that takes up all your fingers. Now again (say it again). Now again faster (same words)." He would keep going until they all could say it together, like a multiplication table. "Children now run home—don't forget what is on your fingers, and tell your parents that a man will preach the gospel tonight at the schoolhouse, as you have it on the five fingers of your hands."[9] Then children would run home, tell their parents about this unique man they met on the playground, and the hall would be packed that night. Many times nearly every house of the village and neighborhood would be represented.[10]

Scott spent some thirty years preaching. He edited several journals, the first of which was called *The Evangelist*. His first book was entitled, *Discourse on the Holy Spirit*. Scott was also the one who had suggested to Campbell to add "Baptist" to the title of Campbell's journal *Christian Baptist*, so that Baptists would read it. Walter Scott also served as the first president of the first brotherhood college, Bacon College, in Georgetown, Kentucky. At his inaugural address at its opening in 1836, Scott said, "Our institution has been denominated 'Bacon College,' in honor of Sir Francis Bacon, that illustrious reformer who contributed so much, by means of his 'Inductive Philosophy' to dispel the mystic science of Aristotle and his followers."[11]

Walter Scott was tireless in his work for the Lord. Mornings often found the energetic Scott at one location, and then evenings at another, miles away. It was common for him to occupy the court-house or schoolhouse in the morning, address a large assembly in some great grove in the afternoon, and then end the day by speaking in a private home crowded with neighbors.[12] Perhaps more than anyone else, Scott found a way to put theory into practice with amazing results.[13] Four years after Scott's death, Moses Lard in his own *Lard's Quarterly*, wrote a piece entitled "Monument to Walter Scott," in which he said, "In two respects only did Walter Scott never become a common man—in profound, exhausting admiration for the Savior and in the love of Truth. Here he will never be excelled."[14] Scott's place among the leaders of the Stone-Campbell Movement is firmly established.

PART TWO: Walter's Heart

Memorization

Walter Scott believed that people needed to memorize Scripture and have it accessible anytime. He directed his students to become thoroughly familiar with the Greek text of the New Testament. He had them commit parts of it to memory, so that they could repeat, chapter by chapter, the whole of the four gospels of Matthew, Mark, Luke, and John in the original language.[15] Scott himself spent part of everyday memorizing and delighting in the Word of God. After he had finished in the classroom, he would often be awake until midnight, studying and learning the text.[16] Some have written that nearly every convert of Scott's became a preacher, either in public or private. Scott wanted every Christian to study the New Testament by day and then meditate on it by night. One of his biographers wrote that scarcely a disciple could be found without a small copy of the "Sacred Oracles" in his pocket as his daily companion. Baxter wrote that these: "numbers had their minds so stored with its truths that they could readily quote from memory whatever the occasion demanded—so much so that they were known as book men, the men of one book, and in a few cases 'walking Bibles.'"[17] Scott encouraged heads of households to memorize the Word. He said, "A chapter per day, will put the head of a family in possession of the entire NT in much less than one year, for there are only 260 chapters in the volume."[18]

Family Bible Study

Scott strongly believed that the home was where the Bible was really taught and put it into practice. His own family devotionals ran typically like this: while breakfast was being prepared, all the family (including even guests who were present), except those who needed to be active in the kitchen, were intensely busy in committing the Scriptures to memory. After breakfast, the first to leave the table and run from the breakfast room to the parlor might be a small child, perhaps two years old. The rest followed, until all were seated in the parlor. They were now gathered for religious instruction. Walter would then give the oldest child, ten years old, a certain look, and the son would sing the song which the children of Israel sang when they were delivered from Egypt. Many were touched by such singing. Next, the father looked over at six-year-old William. This son began completely unembarrassed, "And Naomi took the child and laid it in her bosom, and became nurse to it," quoting from the first part of Ruth in the Old Testament. Then, daughter Emily, eight-years-old, asked her father where they could find the story of Naomi. Scott would answer, "In the book of Ruth." Scott then turned to the rest and said, "What a great book it is. It seems to be in the scriptures because it shows the pedigree of the royal family of David." Next, Emily repeated with hundred percent accuracy the whole of the Messiah's lineage from Adam to Abraham, from Abraham to David, and then from David to Jesus.[19] B. U. Watkins, who stayed one time with the Scotts, wrote later of the experience:

> It was our habit to commit to memory a chapter from the NT before breakfast, each selecting different portions of Scripture, which we recited at family worship, which came directly after eating. In this exercise, each member of the family was expected to take part. . . . After morning worship, it was our custom to walk out together, and during the walk refresh our

> memories with what we had learned in the last week or month. This was done by reciting from memory and prompting each other without the use of any book.[20]

Scott shared a few details of his family study in his journal, *The Evangelist*: "We have got twice through Genesis, and have examined it with maps, and the help of encyclopedias, learned dictionaries, etc. Do I tell you this for the purpose of piping forth our piety? God is our witness that we do not; but to excite you to do the same . . . that you may be partakers of the same refreshing consolations."[21]

Love for the God of Nature

Some of Scott's heart came from living in the picturesque mountains around Eastern Ohio and Western Pennsylvania. On the day he was chosen for elder of the Alleghany church (1848), he wrote in his diary:

> The first day of my eldership. Studied, wrote and walked to the top of the hill north. This is a great exercise for the lungs and limbs. . . . In ascending, we rise from the idea of man's weakness into that of God's power; we ascend from the restlessness of the finite to the tranquility of the infinite. On the hillside I felt myself with God . . . began my descent running, and continued it the whole length of the hill downwards, every muscle of my limbs and body aching in response to the powerful test to which their strength and elasticity were put by the exercise. Sought to reclaim an erring brother. Visited another in reference to a family Bible. Spent the night in study.[22]

A few days later, another entry read:

> With the multitude of hills lying all around me, I could not but lift up my hat as being in the presence of God, "Great and marvelous are thy works, Lord God Almighty; just and true are thy ways, O King of saints." Involuntarily I repeated that

> inimitable inspiration—the 34th Psalm, 'I will bless the Lord at all times, his praise shall be continually in my mouth. . . .' The noise of the city, very audible, ascended from below like the noise of a host preparing for battle. I descended running; the entire length of the hill did not exhaust me. My mouth and muscles, my limbs and lungs stood it admirably. Made twenty or thirty calls. Had some talk both with Irish Catholic and Scotch Presbyterians.[23]

Baxter wrote, "Even in the daily duties of the schoolroom, he led his pupils to similar contemplations, so that they might be induced to look through nature up to nature's God."[24]

One of his students was Robert Richardson, who wrote about his walk with Scott among the gardens. He said of Walter Scott, "Nature, in all its forms, seemed to speak to him only of its Creator." Scott loved learning the names of plants and trees. One time he was out riding with Daniel Hayden, a co-preacher, and asked him, "I want you to tell me the name of that noble tree by the roadside." Hayden replied, "That is a white-oak." Scott turned to his companion and said, "Hold my horse." Scott then leaped to the ground, ran to the tree in question, and plucked off one of its leaves, memorizing both its form and name. We are told that this scene was repeated often whenever he saw a tree whose name he did not know.[25]

Head and Heart

Walter Scott knew that preaching could and should enlighten the mind. He realized that people have to be convinced of certain truths in their heads. David Edwin Harrell believes that "Scott's restored gospel was a distinctly left-brained alternative offered to a population enthralled by the blossoming of science and rational thought."[26] In the same vein, Dwight Bozeman judges Scott's apparent lack of popular spirituality. He states:

> Scott ignored or marginalized the "Spiritual exercises" of preparation for conversion: fasting, systematic introspection, the "watch" over temptations, meditation, spiritual diaries, the catalogue of sins, the quest for "signs and evidence" of a safe estate before God, or daily devotional schedules. He devoted relatively little attention to spirituality and made no effort to formulate a distinctive practice of piety for his new reformation.[27]

Nevertheless, few preachers could make the message as plain and simple and as convicting as Scott. However, once the logic of Scripture was understood, Scott would then drive the point deeper, right to the heart.[28] Scott's power was certainly over both the minds and hearts of the masses. It has been said that his dark eyes seemed to penetrate the secrets of the soul and that his voice was soothing or terrible as he uttered the promises or threats of the Word of God.[29]

Scott's preaching could even move the usually non-excitable Alexander Campbell to issue vocal affirmations. One such event was recorded by R. R. Sloan:

> Walter Scott, about 1829 or 1830, paid a visit to western Virginia, and on one occasion preached in the woods between Wellsburg and Wheeling; the audience was large, the preacher more than usually animated by his theme; near him sat Alexander Campbell, usually calm and self-contained, but in this case more fully under the influence of the preacher's eloquence than he had ever been of mortal man before; his eyes flashed and his face glowed as he heard him unfold the glories of redemption, the dignity and compassion of its author, and the honors that awaited those who would submit to his reign, until so filled with rapture and an admiration, not of the speaker, but of him who was his theme, that he cried out,

"Glory to God in the highest," as the only way to relieve the intensity of his joy.[30]

Scott was not known for extemporaneous sermons. Even so, he could respond appropriately when certain situations demanded it. On one occasion while preaching on the Atonement, he noticed that more than a few of his audience were starting to nod off. He quickly turned his attention to some of the boys on the front row and asked if they knew a game called "Toad Sky High." After learning that they were familiar with the sport, Scott shared his own experience of the game as a youth, where he would lean a wooden plank on a stone, place a toad on one end of the plank, and then with a stick pound on the higher end, sending the frog soaring across the sky. The boys laughed. Then Scott proceeded to tell the boys that the game really was bad, since the unfortunate toad met his death in the game. Scott continued, describing the death of the frog in such detail that the boys were brought to tears. At this point, Scott turned his attention to the rest of his audience, and scolding them by saying, "Your children are weeping over the death of a toad, while you have been sleeping through the story of the death of your Lord!"[31]

Often Scott would accompany younger men on their preaching appointments. It was not uncommon for churches to have two visiting preachers. Accompanying a young preacher to his appointment, Scott informed him, "Now I will tell you how we must do; I will preach, and you must follow in an exhortation; I will strike at the head, and you must strike at the heart."[32]

Scott knew that conversion involved one's whole being. Certainly the occasion when one could witness the dual involvement of Scott's own head and heart was the day he became a United States citizen. Later he described the scene this way:

> I remember distinctly the moment that I became an American citizen in heart; it was not when I went through the forms of the laws of naturalization, but on the occasion of my meeting with a procession headed by a band playing the national air, and bearing the national banner; inspired by the strain as I looked on the national emblem, I felt that under that flag, and for it, if need be, I could die, and I felt at that moment that I was in feeling, as well as in law, an American citizen, that that flag was my flag, and that this country was my country.[33]

Since Walter Scott's sermons typically addressed the whole person, people often remembered single lessons of his for years. In fact, some of his sermons could be recalled by people twenty or more years later.[34]

One individual who heard Walter Scott preach said that Scott was

> middle height, quite erect, well formed, easy and graceful in all his movements; his hair black and glossy, even to advanced age; he had piercing black eyes, which seemed at one time to burn, at another, to melt; his face was a remarkable one, the saddest, or gladdest, as melancholy or joy prevailed; his voice was one of the richest I ever heard, suited to the expression of every emotion of the soul—and when his subject took full

> possession of him he was an orator . . . with face upturned and hand outstretched, he stood describing the scene he really seemed to behold.[35]

Scott possessed an amazing power to bring people into a scene just through the use of carefully chosen vocabulary, gestures, and voice inflections. Baxter wrote, for example, that when Scott preached on the transfiguration of Christ, he described it with such marvelous power that his audience seemed to stand on the mountain with the apostles.[36]

Scott was not always at his best when he came to preaching. He himself admitted it. He was susceptible to illness or bouts of depression. Some have even suspected that Scott suffered from manic-depression.[37] He was heartbroken because of the Civil War. In a letter to his son, he wrote:

> You say: "I am so disheartened and cast down, so overwhelmed with the general gloom that overspreads my dear, my native land, that I can scarcely think of anything else." These words, my son, precisely describe my state of mind. I can think of nothing but the sorrows and dangers of my most beloved adopted country. God is witness to my tears and grief. I am cast down. I am afflicted. I am all broken to pieces. My confidence in man is gone. May the father of mercies show us mercy. Mine eye runneth down with grief.[38]

During those times he thought he could be of more help to the church through writing. However, when he was at his best no one could preach better than Walter Scott. Baxter, Scott's biographer, met with an influential brotherhood preacher long after Scott had died. Baxter asked the man if he had ever seen or heard Walter Scott. The preacher spoke with a degree of sadness in his voice, "Yes." Baxter next asked, "What did you think of him?" "Ah," the preacher said, "For one hour and a half, I was nearer heaven than ever before or since."[39]

The Power of Song

In 1838, Scott published a new hymnal for church use. Originally, it was to be an enlargement of the hymnbook he and Campbell had produced earlier. However, Campbell refused to attach his own name to this new edition until it was approved by a select committee. Scott could not wait that long, so he used three hundred dollars of his own money to get it published and distributed under his own name. His aim through the hymnal was to encourage congregations to stop "the endlessly repeated singing of the same hymn to the same tune, at present so common in our assemblies."[40]

He had been thrilled by the great singing he had experienced on the Western Reserve. He wanted to keep that joyful sound alive. On the whole, Scott thought that Protestants sang badly. In his preface, he offered three reasons why Christians should "cultivate Sacred Music":

> 1st Music is a science, that is, it has its foundation in nature, or like all natural science, it has God for its author.
>
> 2nd It is commanded us to sing. The Holy Spirit enjoins us to "sing and make melody"—a thing which cannot be done aright without some knowledge of music.
>
> 3rd It is the office of a hymn to arouse impassioned devotional feeling, even as it is the office of teaching to illuminate the understanding. [41]

He insisted that sacred music be good music. Scott stated,

> A few old hymns which associate themselves with our earliest and most devout recollections and which are remarkable for their nervous diction, have been corrected and inserted; but we could not bear to stereotype weakness or enthusiasm. There must be strength, feeling, and progression of thought in a hymn.[42]

Scott loved music and enjoyed singing all his life. His father had been an artist and music teacher. Peter Morgan noted that Scott's songs could move audiences to compassion. No doubt Scott remembered his own experience as a youth when he sang beside the blind beggar on the street and witnessed that music, not just information, moved passersby to compassion. Music, therefore, must always accompany evangelistic work, and so Scott frequently traveled with the singing evangelist, song leader, and soloist, William Hayden.

Scott was also a poet and wrote poetry throughout his life. Many times, his sermons would soar on the wings of his own compositions.[43] As noted earlier, Scott often had opportunities to enjoy the beauty of nature around his home and as he traveled. Here is a sample of his poem on the subject of "Stars."

> What are you, Stars? The eyes of heaven?
> Or jewels in God's kingly crown?
> Or gems in his imperial robe?
> Which he at eventide puts on?
> Perhaps you are the military of heaven.
> To whom to guard his state the honor's given.
>
> Perhaps you're golden links that bind
> The sable curtains of the night,
> Or emerald urns, whence flows the die
> That paints them azure when 'tis light;
> Or seraph-sentinels round heaven's height,
> To watch the sleeping world through the night.[44]

Pray Above All Else

Walter Scott wrote in *The Evangelist*:

> Let secret prayer, by yourself alone, be constantly performed before the work of the day be undertaken. It is much better

> to go from prayer to business, than from business to prayer, in regard of the mind's freedom from distracting thoughts. And all, because if the world gets the start of religion in the morning, it is hard for religion to overtake the world all the day after.[45]

In another article, he stated:

> In Jerusalem of old, where the true worship once flourished, there was a morning and evening service. How transporting to the devout Israelites to ascend the hill of God at the hour of prayer...In villages, towns, and cities, this might and perhaps ought to be done. How is it, that Protestants are in this respect excelled by the Catholics and even the Mahommedans? These last people have their hour of morning and evening prayer and never allow themselves to enter upon the business of the day till they have offered the first fruits of the day to God. . . . Let them meet daily in this manner for prayer, and see if God will not pour out a blessing upon you till there be no room to hold it.[46]

Scott knew that prayer was being pushed aside by other cares of the day:

> The practice of calling upon God night and morning in their families is awfully neglected by parents and the heads of houses. There are thousands who never think of such a matter, and this is not the worst of it. There are professing populations of one thousand in which there is not a family that calls upon the Lord night and morning. This matter must no longer be slurred upon. The disciples themselves require to be reformed. The true Gospel is abused by such a profession of it....Christ Jesus is put to an open shame by such professors. The Bible is of course seldom and in some instances never read in such houses and families. . . . Now we entreat our brethren to reform and

> pursue the things, and manners, and customs, that make for their perfection in their most holy profession. Let us be a prayerful and a praying people; let us be full of the spirit of praise. . . . If you will return, God will heal your backsliding and love you freely, He will take away your iniquities and receive you graciously.[47]

Before Scott accepted the invitation to evangelize the Western Reserve, he spent nearly two months in prayer and consultation with other Christians.

The Tribute from Campbell

Walter Scott and Alexander Campbell did not always see eye to eye. Concerning the name which they should call those in the movement, Scott preferred the name "Christian,"[48] while Campbell preferred "Disciple." Campbell never liked Scott's title of one of his books, *The Gospel Restored*. He thought it sounded a bit presumptuous. Despite these differences, Campbell always loved Walter Scott. They were friends for forty years. Walter Scott died on April 23, 1861, at the age of sixty-five. When Campbell received the news of Scott's death, he penned a lengthy eulogy. Reflecting on his memories of Scott, Campbell described him as, "Next to my father my most cordial and indefatigable fellow-laborer in the origin and progress of the present Reformation." Later in the eulogy, he wrote: "I knew him well. I knew him long. I loved him much. We might not, indeed, agree in every opinion nor in every point of expediency; but we never loved each other less because we did not acquiesce in every opinion and in every measure. By the eye of faith and the eye of hope, methinks I see him in Abraham's bosom."[49]

Chapter Three Notes

1. Later, Henry's son, Isaac, would become renowned in the Christian church.

2. This is the same Robert Richardson who would later write *The Memoirs of Alexander Campbell.*

3. William Baxter, *Life of Elder Walter Scott* (Nashville: Gospel Advocate Co., 1875), 57, quotes from Richardson who wrote of this scene fifty years later.

4. Robert Richardson, *Memoirs of Alexander Campbell, embracing a view of the origin, progress and principles of the religious reformation which he advocated* (Cincinnati: Standard Publishing, 1898), 2:199.

5. Walter Scott, *Evangelist* 1 (1832): 94.

6. Dwight E. Stevenson, *Walter Scott: Voice of the Golden Oracle* (Joplin, Mo.: College Press, 1946), 109.

7. Quoted in William A. Gerrard, III, *A Biographical Study of Walter Scott: American Frontier Evangelist* (Joplin, Mo.: College Press, 1992), 123.

8. Ibid., 214.

9. It is interesting that the five steps have gone through some alteration over the years. While Walter Scott placed more emphasis on what God has done, somewhere along the way the five steps were altered, and now many people emphasize only what humans do. "Hear, believe, repent, confess, baptized" are now often quoted as the correct five steps in God's divine plan of salvation. Olbricht contends that it was Isaac Errett was popularized the five-fold plan and emphasized human actions. Thomas H. Olbricht, "The Holy Spirit in the Early Restoration Movement," *Stone Campbell Journal* 7.1 (Spring, 2004): 14, 16. Scott would later add a sixth step, eternal life.

10. Baxter, *Life of Elder Walter Scott*, 185f.

11. Recorded by Charles Crossfield Ware, *Barton Warren Stone: Pathfinder of Christian Union: A Story of His Life and Times* (St. Louis: Bethany, 1932), 287. Incidentally, Bacon College opened five years before Campbell's Bethany College.

12. Baxter, *Life of Elder Walter Scott*, 148.

13. Krause believes that much of Scott's more enlightened paradigm for salvation stems from his contention with rampant Augustinianism found among the Protestant Christians of his day who thought that the Holy Spirit worked miraculously on the heart of the believer to produce faith. Mark Krause, "Five Post-Modern Fingers: Walter Scott for the 21st Century," *Stone Campbell Journal* 7.2 (Fall, 2004): 244.

14. Moses Lard, "Monument to Walter Scott," *Lard's Quarterly* 2 (January, 1865), quoted in Charles Gresham, "An Historical and Bibliographical Note on the Biographical Approaches to Walter Scott," *Stone Campbell Journal* 2.1, (Spring, 1999): 40.

15. Baxter, *Life of Elder Walter Scott*, 58.

16. Ibid., 61.

17. Ibid., 183.

18. Stevenson, *Walter Scott*, 140.

19. Baxter, *Life of Elder Walter Scott*, 247f.

20. Ibid., 250.

21. Scott, *Evangelist* 6 (August 1838): 77.
22. Baxter, *Life of Elder Walter Scott*, 405.
23. Ibid., 407.
24. Ibid., 58.
25. Ibid., 176f.
26. David Edwin Harrell, Jr, "Walter Scott and the Nineteenth-Century Evangelical Spirit," in Mark Toulouse, ed., *Walter Scott: A Nineteenth Century Evangelical* (St. Louis: Chalice Press, 1999), 26.
27. Dwight T. Bozeman, "'Stupendous Facts': Walter Scott's Primitivist Spirituality," in Mark Toulouse, ed., *Walter Scott*, 110-111, 122. Later in the essay Bozeman acknowledges that Scott's religion of Christ was still a religion of both feeling and faith.
28. Ibid., 340.
29. Ibid., 350.
30. Quoted in Baxter, *Life of Elder Walter Scott*, 220.
31. Stevenson, *Walter Scott*, 75-76.
32. Baxter, *Life of Elder Walter Scott*, 257.
33. Ibid., 353.
34. Ibid., 346.
35. Ibid., 343.
36. Ibid., 345.
37. Peter M. Morgan, "Walter Scott: The Artistry of His Ministry," in Toulouse, ed., *Walter Scott*, 5. Fred Craddock also suspects manic-depression. See "Shall We Preach the 'R' Word Again?" in ibid., 138.
38. Ibid., 441.
39. Ibid., 220.
40. Mark Toulouse, "Walter Scott: A Nineteenth-Century Evangelical," in Toulouse, ed., *Walter Scott*, 17.
41. Stevenson, *Walter Scott*, 175; Walter Scott, *Christian Psalms and Hymns* (Louisville, KY: J. Maxwell, Jr., 1839).
42. Ibid., 176.
43. Morgan, "Walter Scott," 4.
44. Quoted in Stevenson, *Walter Scott*, 20-21.
45. Scott, *Evangelist* 9 (August, 1841): 191.
46. Ibid. (May, 1840): 109.
47. Scott, "Non-Worship Families," *Evangelist* 8 (April 1, 1840) 4, 89, 90.
48. Evidenced in a conversation with John Smith, cited in John Augustus Williams, *Life of Elder John Smith* (Cincinnati: R.W. Carroll, 1870), 541-545.
49. Alexander Campbell, "Elder Walter Scott's Demise," *Millennial Harbinger* 4th series, no. 3 (1861): 297.

Chapter Four

JOHN ROGERS

Preacher on Horseback

PART ONE: John's Story (1800-1867)

Rough Methodist Roots

In the last month and on the sixth day of the new century of 1800 John was born in Clarke County, Kentucky to Ezekiel and Rebecca Rogers. A few years earlier they had migrated from Virginia looking for land and new opportunities. Rebecca had been a long time member of the Methodist Episcopal Church. John referred to her as an "Immersed Methodist"[1] and she stayed one all her life. Ezekiel had also been a very devout Methodist for a few years, even a class leader, but then left the faith. John remembered his older brother talking about his father's story and hearing him say that his dad felt it was his duty to preach the gospel to sinners. Yet, because of a poor education, he did not feel himself qualified. So the father chose not to preach, and finally became a skeptic. He had also begun reading Thomas Paine's *Age of Reason* and similar works. So, when middle aged, his father gave up Christianity altogether. John only knew his father as a hard-working farmer. He wrote in his autobiography that if his father had not fallen into the habit of drinking he might have made something of himself and his family. Ezekiel Rogers died when John was ten years old. Reportedly, he had created some kind of trouble with one of the locals, who pursued him through three states. Finally, the man caught up with his father and beat him to death with a club.

John was the youngest of eight children (four girls and four boys). For his first seventeen years, he had no religious experience at all. Looking back, he wrote that he never even heard a sermon or felt any interest in Christianity during those years. Then in 1817, as the great revivals were making their way across Kentucky, one took place in nearby Concord. It was led by elders Reuben Dooley, James Hughes, Barton Stone, and others. John's brother Samuel and Samuel's wife were converted, as well as two of the sisters. John was impressed that his older brother Samuel, who had once lived life on the wild side, soon "commenced preaching." Samuel Rogers preached for over forty years.

Concerning these revivals, John only heard about most of them. His job as an indentured cabinet maker prevented him from attending most of these meetings. By contract, he had to stay with his employers for six years until he was twenty-one years old. Still, he was curious about these unique happenings, and managed to slip away a few times and investigate them for himself. The revivals were the biggest news in Kentucky at the time. Here John saw firsthand people fainting, jerking, dancing, and engaging in all the other strange bodily "exercises." He wrote of these, saying that even though there were "all these disorders, there was much piety and deep religious feeling."[2]

If his religious opportunities had been small for his first seventeen years, so were his opportunities for education. He stated that the sum of his learning when he entered his trade was that he could read and write and do his multiplication tables through the threes.[3] Nonetheless, his appetite for education was growing. During the initial three years of apprenticeship, as he would slip out to observe the revivals, he also used this more leisurely time to read anything on which he could get his hands. A new physician moved to town and discovered John's thirst for knowledge. He brought him all kinds of new books and things he thought might be beneficial to one's education.

John's apprenticeship continued. During that time, he also picked up a few habits of which he would later repent and give up. He had started playing cards and gambled a little. He also took up billiards and he would play until long into the night. Rogers wrote in his autobiography, "Where these habits of gaming might have led me, but for the favor of God which stopped me in my wild career, and turned me about, God only knows."[4]

Conversion without the Experience

In 1818, Barton Stone began coming to Millersburg, Kentucky, where Rogers was now living. There were also several Baptist preachers coming through the area. Rogers went to hear all of them. At age eighteen, John decided he would seek religion. Part of the Baptist conversion meant having a spiritual experience. Presbyterians also encouraged people to share their conversion narratives. In fact, anyone seeking full admission to a frontier church was required to offer these personal narratives as evidence of their regeneration.[5] This meant that people literally had to "seek religion." Most Baptists in the early nineteenth century were strong Calvinists, much more so than they are now. Calvin's theology included "double predestination." God, before history began, decided who would go to heaven and who would go to hell. Nothing one did would alter God's determined fate. One could only seek to discover it. The method of discovery meant having some religious experience. Following this, one related his/her story to a local Baptist group which would then vote the prospective member into their fellowship. This was the message John Rogers was hearing. He recalled being exhorted to pray more and to look to God for some inexplicable, sensible manifestation. All he lacked was the tangible experience whereby he would know that he was numbered among the elect and his sins were erased. For some, it might mean something as simple as being out in the wagon one day and while riding, a tree would fall across the path, perhaps startling one's horse. But upon reflection, this person knew that if he had come across that path two seconds later, he or his horse might have been crushed. Such a close call in all probability meant that God was demonstrating which camp the individual was in. It was a small but very clear sign that one was among the chosen.

John Rogers recalled hearing a Methodist preacher preach in the fall of 1818. The message brought John's heart closer to God. Yet he had not had the experience. The preacher's words only made him weep. So he went out to the nearby woods by himself and prayed. He spent the whole night in tears over his sins, trying to pray. But John said that his prayers seemed to go no higher than his own head.[6] He returned to town, still a seeker. God had not yet granted him the valid experience.

He went to hear more preachers. It did not matter whether God's spokesperson were Baptist, Methodist, or another persuasion. The name did not matter. He was a sponge, soaking up all the religious information he could. He prayed routinely twice a day. He attended more meetings, asking for prayers from the preachers and from anyone who would pray for him. But still he complained, "that electric shock, that non-descript operation, by which I should know I was a new man, that my sins had been forgiven" never came.[7]

Finally, on one occasion he attended a Baptist prayer meeting. Rogers remembered that during that particular meeting the congregation sang a very beautiful and, in his case, a very appropriate hymn, and it spoke to his condition. The words were as follows:

Sinner, hear the Saviors call,
He is now passing by;
He has seen thy grievous thrall,
And hears thy mournful cry.

The last verse especially got his attention.

Raise thy downcast eyes and see
What throngs his throne surround.
These, tho' sinners once like thee,
Have full salvation found.

Yield not then to unbelief,
While he says there yet is room,
Tho' of sinners thou are chief,
Since Jesus calls thee, come.[8]

Rogers was now convinced that God had indeed sent his divine mercy. When the congregation finished the singing of that hymn, Rogers spoke out, "Let us pray." The congregation dropped to their knees. Rogers said there was a death-like silence as they all prayed with him. He felt himself paralyzed with fear. He said, "Every idea forsook me." Still he tried to pray the best he could. This was his first real public prayer. Others felt the conviction of God as he prayed. Just a short time after that meeting, John Rogers was baptized by immersion by Barton Stone and joined one of the churches associated with the growing Stone movement.

Early Years of Preaching

For a youth of just eighteen, joining the Stone movement was a brave step. They were calling themselves, "Christian Church," believing they stood on the truth. All his other close friends had joined the Baptists. Rogers wrote in his autobiography: "I, solitary and alone, against the remonstrances of all my associates and all the sects, who spoke of Stone and his positions in terms of the strongest reprobation, united with that sect everywhere spoken against."[9]

Nonetheless, Rogers was convinced he was in the right camp. He was also convinced that the world needed the Lord. He felt overwhelmed by the task. He was aware of his own inadequacy and lack of training. Moreover, he was still stuck in a three-year apprenticeship making cabinets. There was no legal way to escape it.

John's older brother Samuel came to the rescue. Since their father had died, Samuel, as older brother, had been appointed John's guardian. He was thrilled to know that young John wanted to preach. Samuel himself was already preaching. Samuel's idea was to sell off part of John's property inheritance for $200. Then he would buy out the rest of John's three-year contract. The plan saw success and John was released. John returned to live with his mother. He recalled later that he wanted to stay there a long time, to "linger among the scenes of his youth."[10] Yet he knew he had to move on.

In late winter of 1819 John set out with Samuel for the older brother's residence in Clinton County, Ohio. At the door John's mother blessed him and lent him her horse. On the way, John remembered stopping for one of Samuel's preaching appointments at Kentontown. That evening Samuel let his younger brother do the preaching. John wrote later: "There for the first time in my life, a mere boy, a little over eighteen, attempted publicly to speak a word in behalf of Christianity. I only distinctly remember that I was very much embarrassed."[11] The following night, John got to preach again near Minerva, Kentucky.

For six months John stayed with Samuel. He also took a job assisting a local cabinet maker. He attended all the church meetings he could, both morning and evening. He would give short talks and pray in the service whenever there was opportunity, all the while seeking more and more time with the Scriptures.

John's employer was not a Christian and not a believer at all. Yet, he was honest and John liked him. He liked his boss's heart and mind. Furthermore, the employer treated John less like a hired hand and more like a brother or son. His boss called John, "My preacher," owing to the fact that whenever possible John would try to shift the conversation into something religious. This man made such an impact on John Rogers that he wrote about him forty-two years later, and said as far as he knew that good man never came to the Lord.[12]

After a few months, Samuel took John away for some extended meetings. They traveled across several counties of Ohio and into Indiana. During that trip John met with several influential preachers of his time. He traveled for a few months on foot, carrying his few clothes the best he could. After a while some friends offered to help him purchase a horse. However, the animal came without a saddle. So John had to return to his former job of making cabinets, at least long enough to save up enough money for a saddle and a bridle. It would take him at least two days to travel back to his former boss's place. Along the way he stopped at a tavern. It was the only place around to stay for the night. He was still eighteen years old, and was used to praying with others before he went to bed. Because he was among strangers, however, he had to muster enough nerve to ask his hosts if he could read Scripture and pray with their family. They saw nothing wrong with it, and so he read them a chapter, prayed, and then went on to bed. It is never known if John ever saw them again, but this unusually mature teenager must have made an impact.

Finally, he worked long enough for his former boss to purchase a saddle. One of the neighboring Christians gave him a set of old saddle-bags. John commented that they looked as if they had been through the Revolutionary War.[13] John accepted the gift graciously. He was now prepared for the ministry of a traveling circuit preacher, the common method of ministers in that time. Then during the late summer of that same year, 1819, he attended a large camp meeting not far from Richmond, Indiana. It was held out in the lush woods near the White Water River. These meetings brought together several congregations, numerous preachers, and interested people from all over the countryside. The meetings would continue for several days and nights, usually until the food supply ran out. John's memory of this particular one was that the "people seemed very unfeeling and at times behaved very badly."[14] He realized that many had

come just for a good time rather than to draw closer to God. When the last morning of the meeting came, before the public service commenced, John ventured back into the woods, poured his heart out in prayer, and asked God to touch the souls of those who had come to the meeting. He then returned to the stand. One preacher spoke his message and the meeting was about to break up. John could sit still no longer. He had to say something. As John remembered it, he preached just a short message, but he released feelings that could not be contained. The sermon was full of deep emotion. He wept as he preached and exhorted. The result was the answer to his prayer. John suddenly noticed the other preacher bathed in tears, others weeping openly. John said later of that experience, "I was a beardless boy, not nineteen years old."[15] Yet his words had cut even the hardened sinners to the heart.

John came down from the stand and, as was the custom, invited people to come forward. John said that he had never before witnessed such a scene. A great throng of people crowded around him, all bathed in tears, all falling upon their knees in the dust before the Lord. Estimates were that around fifty came forward on that occasion. John wrote that the other preacher came over, hugged him, and told him to always be faithful and humble, and keep on studying the Word of God, to keep preaching Jesus Christ and him crucified. The preacher also prayed that John might live long on the earth, and build up the cause of Christ.[16]

Ordination at Last

Not long after, John Rogers attended another revival meeting in Warren County, Ohio. Like most other revivals, it was held in the woods. A quick platform was erected on which speakers could stand. Its height was about three or four feet, its length was ten feet, and its width five or six feet. A board was placed across the front of it on which the speaker could rest a book. On this occasion a large audience was present. It probably numbered in the hundreds. Rogers mentioned that his brother Clarke was to be the preacher and he, John, the exhorter.[17] Walter Scott had told his young associate that he would preach first, convince the head; and then the younger preacher should strike at the heart. At this meeting Rogers said that many preachers were present. Several of them, in Rogers' words, were "men of age, ability and learning." Young John Rogers was by no means a confident, polished speaker yet. In fact, though he would preach for forty years, he never felt at ease while preaching. Rogers related that brother Clarke preached that day without much embarrassment. John sat behind him, trembling the whole time. He wrote later that he remembered standing up, but he had no memory of what he said. He recorded, "[I was] young, beardless, ignorant, but my heart was full of the great theme of redemption." He was still less than nineteen years old. Without any memory of his words, Rogers did remember that suddenly the camp was on fire with feeling. Two preachers started shouting at the tops of their voices, dancing while they were shouting. Then within a few minutes, the whole area in front of the stand was filled with men and women dancing and shouting. Rogers was so taken aback that he was left speechless. He stopped preaching, and decided to let someone else take over. Rogers wrote, "I had not attempted to preach, but I received license at that conference to exercise my talents in 'such a way as God may direct.'"[18]

Years later Rogers reflected on what happened that evening. He knew that most people in the movement would probably frown on what occurred that night, with its excessive enthusiasm. He stated that some might even call it disgusting and claim that there was no true piety there at all. However, Rogers cautioned, one should not be so fast to judge or condemn. He knew that people in those times and regions were different than later in the century. These people were probably less enlightened in doctrine. At the same time, he said that he doubted if his contemporary readers possessed as much piety and spirituality as did these camp attendees.

As the snow fell in the winter of 1819, Rogers began attending the school in Georgetown, Kentucky, where Barton Stone was teaching. Stone saw promise in John and provided for his tuition. John decided to make the most of his time. While there, he went to all the meetings and revivals he could attend, "all within reach," all the while sharpening his own preaching skills. It was a time of deepening conviction and devotion. He also had opportunity to meet several young preachers similar in age and ability. Barton Stone had brought many of these into the faith and had taught them. By 1820, Stone signed John Rogers' ordination papers. The document read:

> The elders of the Christian Church assembled at Minerva, April 10, 1820, have unanimously ordained our brother, John Rogers, to the ministry of the Gospel, according to the will of God, our Savior, by the commendation of the Christian Church at Georgetown, in which he has lived and labored for some time past.
>
> Signed by the order of the Elders.
> BARTON W. STONE, E.C.C.[19]

Riding the Circuit on Horseback

Rogers then began his full-time preaching work. In this time, no preacher was involved in a single local work only, but spread the message to several congregations in a "circuit." Following the advice of some senior preachers, John set up his own circuit that took him to several towns throughout Kentucky. Looking back, Rogers said that there were only about two meeting houses in the whole circuit. The rest of the meetings were held in private homes or at stands in the woods in warmer

weather. Also like most preachers, he wished he would have kept better records of those early years. However, one experience that he never forgot was his first baptism of a convert. It happened in the summer of 1820. He had spoken to a large crowd out in the woods by a creek. At the conclusion of his sermon, eleven came forward asking for baptism. The difficulty was that the water nearby was just a creek. He knew from his own studies and convictions that he had to immerse them. Rogers wrote that some of them "were quite large, and the water was rather shallow." He never wrote how he accomplished the task. All he said was that "it was quite a trial to one so young and inexperienced as I."[20]

Rogers would go on to baptize four or five thousand people. Moreover, he participated in some of the great 1820 camp meetings in Kentucky, when huge masses of people came from several counties, in wagons, on horseback, or on foot. Usually the day began with people gathering before breakfast for prayer and singing. After breakfast, they assembled to hear preaching from ten to eleven a.m. The crowds met again in the afternoon around two or three o'clock for more preaching, singing, exhortation, and prayer. This was followed by a return to one's wagon or tent for the evening meal. Those who lived close enough went to their homes for supper, while the rest had the meal on the grounds. However, the day was not yet completed. The crowds met once more for the night services, where again there would be preaching, singing, and prayer.

Rogers knew that these meetings were not as orderly as they could be, and things would occasionally get out of hand. Many times there would be a great deal of "wildfire enthusiasm." He wrote:

> Still in very many there existed deep piety, the purest devotion to God and benevolence to man, illustrated in the most animated and heart-searching appeals from the pulpit, the most fervent and earnest prayer for the salvation of sinners, and singing – the most feeling and soul-stirring—all backed by a life of purity . . . presenting altogether quite a contrast with the coldness and elegant formalism of these times. Those were times of refreshing and I highly enjoyed them.[21]

On New Year's Day, 1822, John married Eleanor, a young woman from Virginia. John remembered that he first saw Eleanor when he attended her father's funeral. Barton Stone was officiating at the service. The attraction must have been instantaneous. Not many days went by before he made her mother's house a regular preaching spot on his circuit. Within just a short while he baptized her mother and the other sisters. This little group was the nucleus of what later became a church.

Being a married man, however, Rogers cut back on his preaching tours and took up a trade to support himself and his new wife. Rogers wrote that, at the time he married Eleanor, he owned one horse, a few clothes, and about seven and a half dollars. Eleanor possessed little more. An inventory of her possessions included an old bureau, a bedstead, a featherbed, some bedclothes, a cow, and a few other miscellaneous items. When guests stopped by, John and Eleanor would lay out some pallets for beds. Sometime later, they obtained an extra bed frame, a straw bed, and then divided the feathers in half to make two featherbeds out of it. John said unashamedly, "Now we feel like we're getting up in the world."[22]

For the next ten years, John continued his trade during the week and preached on the weekends. He never took any money for his preaching. Eleanor later died of tuberculosis, and only one of her children lived many years beyond her, all dying quite young. Frontier life took its toll. John's second wife was Mildred who was always a great encourager in his preaching.

Promoter of Unity

For several years John Rogers worked in the same area as Barton Stone. Later when the Stone and Campbell movements united in Georgetown, Kentucky (1832), he played a key role. Rogers (from the Stone side) set out with "Raccoon" John Smith (from Campbell's side) and rode from town to town. Whenever they found two churches (one from Stone's group and one from Campbell's) in the same town, they encouraged them to meet together. He wrote later of that 1832 event, "The importance of that union has never been appreciated, and perhaps cannot be yet. It will be hereafter, when we who were the actors in it shall have passed away."[23]

Rogers preached about forty years, until his death in 1867. The following year, "Raccoon" John Smith (then eighty-four years old) attended a district meeting in Missouri. Someone handed him a picture of John Rogers. Raccoon took the image in his shaking hand and studied it quietly before he spoke. He said: "I knew him well. We labored together in bringing about a union of the Reformers and those called Christians. He was one of the purest men I have ever known in this Reformation. I have never allowed any man to say aught against the character of John Rogers. He's gone to his reward, and I will soon follow him."[24] It may be the case that Rogers' greatest contribution was in helping to affect the union that might never have happened without his tireless efforts in seeing it to fruition. For at least three years in church after church, in meeting after meeting, his continual message was, "We are now a united people!"

PART TWO:
John's Heart

A Sure Conversion

According to the current Calvinist doctrine, Rogers sought an experience of his divine election. He sought it for months, praying, weeping, and looking for any sign that he was one of God's chosen and thereby saved. In his autobiography, he asked, "Why did I—why do many others—seek religion, or seek pardon, for months, without obtaining it, or a satisfactory evidence of it? This is a question of immense practical interest, and a scriptural answer to it, recognized by the different religious parties, and acted upon, would introduce a new era in the history of the modern church."[25]

Rogers believed that a new era had, in fact, come to the church. When he wrote the above lines he had already looked into the answer through "the light of the gospel" for twenty-five years. In his view, one must contend with several facts. He stated that among these were:

1. Very many who profess to be Christians, and give "clear evidence of piety" were seeking religion, or the evidence of their acceptance with God for days, weeks, months, sometimes even years.
2. Although they had the teaching and the prayers of the "most orthodox and evangelical ministers," still it was long before they found peace, or to use their phrase, "got through" or "got religion."
3. These persons, even after they obtained comfort, were often thrown into doubt. Maybe, they thought, they had been mistaken.
4. The orthodoxy of the day encouraged the idea that penitents were to expect some mystical impulse, or "touch of the Spirit" to give them evidence of their forgiveness. "All this revival machinery is put into requisition to move Jehovah to send his Spirit to speak the sentence of pardon in the conscience of true penitents. What a burlesque upon the wisdom and benevolence of God!"
5. This false position gave rise to certain phraseology. The most pious and sober-minded individuals speak of their

> "hope." It is their "hope" that God, for Christ's sake, has forgiven their sins. [26]

Rogers commented that even the "talented and pious" Dr. MacKnight thought, "We shall never know we are pardoned till the last judgment." John Newton, author of "Amazing Grace," penned similar lines:

> 'Tis a point I long to know;
> Oft it causes anxious thought;
> Do I love the Lord or no?
> Am I his, or am I not?[27]

These five facts, Rogers believed, had led even the most pious and orthodox into anxiety and uncertainty. This was completely different from Paul in the New Testament who wrote with conviction and certainty about his salvation. To Titus, Paul spoke of God "who has saved us."[28] In Ephesians, Paul exulted, "By grace you are saved."[29] To Christians in several places, Paul wrote of "being justified freely by his grace"[30] and "redemption in the blood of Christ."[31] Paul was not alone in his convictions. The apostle John in his letter encouraged Christians to "know you are saved."[32]

Rogers believed that early Christians knew they were forgiven. Nowhere could he find the language of doubt or fear on the subject. Rogers knew that this was at variance with facts three and five mentioned above. Concerning facts one and four, that people should expect some kind of mystical experience, Rogers related that this was not the case in the first century. In that time people never had to agonize or wrestle with the issue for weeks, months, or years, nor ask others to pray for them. Rogers was convinced of the clarity in Scripture. Peter, during the Jewish festival of Pentecost in the book of Acts, never had the 3,000 convicted souls to come forward and ask for prayers of the apostles. They were not required to wait until God sent down his Spirit to convert them and give them some evidence of their forgiveness, so that they could then be baptized and received into the church. Rogers was emphatic as he asked, "Did any one of the apostles, or evangelists of the New Reign, ever do it? Never—unequivocally never!"[33] Indeed, first-century believers were never forced to wait days, weeks, or longer to "get through" or "get religion."[34]

Instead, John Rogers said that in the days of the apostles all sincere persons who repented, without exception, would receive immediate relief when they were baptized. He analyzed Acts 2:38, saying, "Peter, the man with the keys, said 'Repent and be baptized, every one of you, in the name of Jesus the Christ, for the remission of sins. Then they that gladly received the word were baptized, and the same day were added unto them about three thousand souls."[35] When that first day of the new church ended, no one was around still seeking. In truth, everybody who was seeking life found it! Rogers said that this was true throughout the remainder of the book of Acts. He cited the cases of the Ethiopian eunuch, the Philippian jailer, and the people who heard the message in Corinth. The text said plainly, "Hearing, they believed and were baptized."[36] Additionally, Rogers felt that it just made good sense that whatever gospel was preached to those first believers to give them immediate relief, this same gospel message should be preached in our time. He yearned for the day when more sincerely religious and pious people would just look calmly at the facts of Scripture and then join together with others who also just read Scripture without wearing the glasses of former interpretations.

When reflecting on his own conversion, he knew that he took a courageous step when all of his other friends were joining the Baptists. He decided to unite with the "Christian Church," thinking that Barton Stone's group and those with him were preaching truth. Much later, Rogers wrote that he did not understand very much of truth then. After all, he was a mere eighteen years old and lacked the competence to judge all their positions. Twenty-five years later, Rogers wrote that he had learned a lot since the beginning. He felt that everything he had learned came to him from his stance (learned from Stone) that the Bible was the only "infallible way."[37] In an 1844 letter to Stone's journal,[38] Rogers said that the first lesson Stone taught him was the all-sufficiency of Scripture as the only rule of faith and practice. This was to be the only basis of Christian union. Rogers truly believed that all party names and creeds were not only anti-scriptural but tended towards schism.

Rogers also wrote that he had learned that "God is love, that he who dwells in love, dwells in God, and God in him." Describing his earlier feelings, he reflected, "My young heart bounded with love to God, the church and the world. I wept over the schisms among Christians. I sighed over a world lying in darkness." His choice, he wrote, was to do nothing but preach. Preaching, he believed, was not to scare off people from hell, but to help them realize the condition of their own hearts. In short, Rogers could no nothing else. He had to preach.

Humility of Soul and Church

Roger's biographer described him as a man of much gravity and seriousness. John enjoyed time with his friends, but was not known for joke telling or being very demonstrative. Likely some of that came from his upbringing and environment. His father had been murdered when John was ten years old. Accordingly, he tended to look towards the more serious side of things. One example was when he was eight years old. He was already living with his uncle, and helping in the mill. By custom, field workers would shell corn at night. The corn would next be prepared for transporting to the local mill, usually by horseback the next day. A large wagon sheet was spread out on a slab or dirt floor, usually in front of a fireplace. The corn itself would be placed on the large sheet and the whole family would sit around and shell the corn. One evening, while everyone was shelling, John's uncle looked over and saw John wiping and rubbing his eyes. Evidently, he had been crying. The uncle asked John what was wrong. John looked up from his work and said, "I was thinking about going to the mill tomorrow and on the way there when I go up that big hill, my sack will fall off, and then hogs would come and eat the corn, before I get anyone to help me, and put it back on my horse again."[39] Young John had apparently been imagining the long list of things that could go wrong. Later, we are told that whenever the uncle noticed John turning a bit too serious, he would tell him, "John, the sack is falling off—you're climbing the hill before you get there." Rogers' biographer related: "But when he did reach the hill and grappled with the real obstacles in the way, no one was more manly, more courageous! While not so hopeful or buoyant as some ministers, where circumstances required it, he was boldly aggressive, even uncompromising."[40]

Rogers took his profession of the Lord Jesus with utter seriousness. Even when he was preaching those sermons at age eighteen, he was aware that he was discussing life and death issues. He knew that people's eternal destinies hung on their response to what they heard. He preached for four decades, and always said he was a bit embarrassed to go before a crowd. Few, however, could persuade people with such force as John Rogers. We are told that he had a strong voice. One said that it had a melody about it and was always under control.[41] Rarely did he say things that he later wished he had not. Although he was not as eloquent as Campbell or as well trained as Stone, Scott, or others, he was always thoughtful about what left his mouth.

John Rogers was also a man of the frontier. For many years his energies were focused on basic frontier survival, with little time for education. Even though he developed a great love for reading, books were few and training was expensive. He had simple wishes. He believed that the message preached should be the uncomplicated gospel message, uncluttered with fruitless discussions or speculations. He knew that people could easily get sidetracked into issues not central to the gospel. Such issues were not only dangerous to the individual, they were also not in the best interests of Christianity.[42]

He wanted his church to be a humble church. In 1829, he sent an article to the *Christian Messenger* in which he said:

> The fatal error of all reformers has been that they have too hastily concluded they knew the whole truth, and have settled back upon the same principles of proscription, intolerance and persecution, against which they so strongly remonstrated in those from whom they seceded. . . . We have no reason to conclude, we know all the truth.
>
> Let us, therefore, acting upon the holy principles we have espoused, always be open to conviction—and thus endeavor to grow in grace, and in knowledge of the truth. We have nothing to lose in this inquiry after truth. We have no system to bind us to human opinions. . . . The better we understand and practice the Bible, the more useful and happier we'll be.[43]

Sweet Singer of Music

John Rogers loved a good song. He had a special passion for hearing others sing. He was also one of the few early preachers in the Stone Campbell movement who could sing well. Some felt that they could almost hear the sound of John's own soul as he sang.[44] Rogers liked new songs and learned them quickly. However, his biographer records that John really enjoyed the older songs, those that could carry him back to earlier times. These were the melodies and lyrics that stirred up memories of former events and associations.

He assisted Campbell in producing church hymnals. On one occasion he mentioned a particular song to Campbell, thinking it might be an excellent song for congregational use. Campbell said that he had never heard the song and asked John to sing it. John proceeded to sing it in his beautifully gifted voice. When he finished, he asked Campbell, "Well, how do you like it?" Campbell answered, "O it is, Brother Rogers, a very fine soliloquy, very fine indeed."[45] Rogers, of course, thought this was a rather peculiar answer. From then on, Rogers felt that, while Campbell's judgment on other matters might be exceptional, he really knew little about songs or the use of melody.

Keep the Heart with the Head

John Rogers' mentality had clearly been molded from an era of wildly emotional revivals. Yet as he came into further contact with Stone, and especially with Campbell, he became increasingly aware that they frowned on this type of behavior People were, in fact, letting their emotions get the best of them. To some extent Rogers excused these people. After he had been in the movement for a few decades, he would say, "That was their time. We know a lot more truth than they knew back then. We now have more light on some important subjects than they had. Yet, they still had something many of us lack." He labeled it "piety and spirituality." He knew that though they were confused about some things, their devotion to Jesus was greater than many in the present movement. Although we know what Scripture really says about conversion, he said, "Let's not judge and condemn them so quickly . . . . If they were upon the extreme of enthusiasm, we are on the extreme of cold formality." Rogers sent a letter to Alexander Campbell in 1834 which said, "Many of us, in running away from the extreme of enthusiasm, have, on the other hand, passed the temperate zone, and gone far into the frozen regions." He wrote, "There is in too many churches, a cold-hearted, lifeless formality that freezes the energies."[46] Perhaps in the attempt to avoid the excesses of what was definitely a misinformed approach to Christianity, the current movement had thrown out emotion altogether. What remained, in Rogers' estimation, was a correct but heartless Christianity. A logical presentation of the facts may be accurate, but without the accompanying heart, even true facts lie powerless. The Lord desires his people to be fully converted.

True First-Century "Reformation"

In 1832 Rogers wrote a letter to Stone's *Christian Messenger.* The letter began by saying that he had just completed a preaching tour. He listed all the places and counties to which he had been. He had often sent similar reports to the *Messenger.* However, this time he chose to share with Stone's readers what his message had been among the churches. He recorded that his message had emphasized personal reformation,

> not consisting merely in a return to primitive order of worship in the congregation, but in a return to the primitive holiness of heart and life. . . . Those breathings of the soul after the mind that was in Christ; to that spirit of humble, fervent, constant prayer to him whose eyes are over the righteous, and whose ears are open to their prayers; and that spirit of deep concern for the conversion of the world. . . . . This characterized the first Christians.

Then he concluded, "Ah, this is the reformation we want. And I state with pleasure, that I found the churches alive to this subject."[47]

Chapter Four Notes

1. John's Rogers autobiographical sketch is included in W. C. Rogers, *Recollections of Men of Faith* (1889; reprint ed., Rosemead, Calif.: Old Paths Book Club, 1960), 138.
2. W. C. Rogers, *Recollections*, 140
3. Ibid., 141.
4. Ibid., 142.
5. John Mark Hicks, "God's Sensible Pledge: Witness of the Spirit in the Early Baptismal Theology of Alexander Campbell," *Stone Campbell Journal* 1 (Spring, 1998): 5.
6. W. C. Rogers, *Recollections*, 143.
7. Ibid.
8. Ibid., 144.
9. John Rogers, *The Biography of Elder Barton Warren Stone written by himself with additions and reflections* (Cincinnati: J.A. and U. P. James, 1847), 153.
10. W. C. Rogers, *Recollections*, 154.
11. Ibid.
12. Ibid., 159.
13. Some forty years earlier.
14. W. C. Rogers, *Recollections*, 166.
15. Ibid., 167.
16. Ibid.
17. Ibid., 171.
18. Ibid., 172.
19. John Rogers said that "E.C.C." stood for Elder of the Church of Christ. Ibid., 179. At the time they were using both names, "Church of Christ" and "Christian Church." As individuals, they referred to themselves always as "Christians."
20. Ibid., 181.
21. Ibid., 182.
22. Ibid., 189.
23. Ibid., 164.
24. Ibid., 206.
25. Ibid., 145f.
26. Ibid., 146.
27. Quoted by W. C. Rogers, *Recollections*, 146.
28. Titus 3:5.
29. Ephesians 2:8.
30. Romans 3:24.
31. Ephesians 1:7.
32. 1 John 5:13.
33. W. C. Rogers, *Recollections*, 148.
34. Ibid., 149.
35. Ibid.
36. Acts 18:8.
37. W. C. Rogers, *Recollections*, 153.

38. *Christian Messenger* 14 (1844): 106.
39. W. C. Rogers, *Recollections*, 198.
40. Ibid.
41. Hughes, *Reviving the Ancient Faith: The Story of Churches of Christ in America* (1996; 2nd edition, Abilene, Tex.: Abilene Christian University Press), 196.
42. Ibid., 197.
43. John Rogers, "The Church of Christ at Concord, to the Elders and Brethren Assembled in Conference at Caneridge, Sendeth Salutation," *Christian Messenger* 4 (October, 1830): 258.
44. W. C. Rogers, *Recollections*, 198.
45. Ibid., 199.
46. Quoted in Leonard Allen, *Distant Voices: Discovering a Forgotten Past for a Changing Church* (Abilene, Tex.: ACU Press, 1993), 79.
47. *Christian Messenger* 6 (1832): 104.

Chapter Five

"RACCOON" JOHN SMITH

Unifier of All Lights

PART ONE:
"Raccoon's" Story (1784-1868)

Surviving Poverty

Sometimes extreme poverty can produce extraordinary people. Such can be said of "Raccoon" John Smith, born on October 15, 1784, in Sullivan County, East Tennessee. The log cabin in which he was reared had three books: a Bible, a Confession of Faith, and a hymn book. The Smith family had struggled not only for education, but for survival itself. When word came of new and cheaper land in the Stockton Valley of Kentucky, the family moved. The new area was sparsely populated. At times, it seemed almost too sparse. One time John's father sent him a hundred miles on horseback to get some corn seed for planting. The youth, only twelve years old, had to swim swollen streams and stay in other log cabins owned by hospitable strangers and friends along the way, but he completed the mission.

Education advantages were non-existent in those regions. If a family was lucky they might snag an occasional wandering schoolteacher who traveled through the wilderness and stopped at individual cabins. When John was eight, he received about four months of education and learned to read. Thereafter, he was often asked to read the Bible on Sundays for worship in their home. A few years later, he enrolled in a private school where again he was taught by a traveling teacher. However, this teacher turned out to be an alcoholic as well as a fraud. One time John showed his dislike of the teacher by pouring a shovel full of hot embers into the teacher's back pocket as he was sitting drunk before the class. Of course, this ended the temporary school, and John got only a slight reprimand at home.

Unique Ordination

When John was nineteen, his father died. It was the year 1803, the same year that his restless heart began to reach out to God. He loved going into the nearby forest where he would literally cry out for salvation. John informed his mother that he earnestly wanted to be a Christian. She answered, "Just wait on the Lord, John."[1] The following year, on the day after Christmas, he appeared before the Baptist church and gave a simple statement about his religious struggles. Impressed by his sincerity, the church voted and the next day he was baptized.

After being admitted into the Baptist church, John wanted more than to be just a Christian spectator. He really wanted to preach. Already he had been attending the cabin meetings of Baptists who frequently gathered for singing and praying. When an ordained minister was absent, someone else with a "natural gift" was asked to exhort. During those times, Smith gained his proficiency for singing and praying, but was reluctant to speak.[2] The problem for him, as he saw it, was that he had not yet received God's direct call to the ministry. So, again in the evenings, he would cry out in agony, pleading with God to give him some unmistakable sign that he should preach the Word of God. He looked everywhere for some tell-tale sign that God wanted to use him in such a profession. One time he came across a rattlesnake that should have bitten him, but did not. Perhaps this was a sign. Another time he narrowly escaped being gored by a vicious bull. Was God speaking again?[3] The rest of the congregation tried to encourage him, "John, you preach even without a direct call."[4] So, with some reluctance, he agreed to make a talk. At the first meeting where he had agreed to give the evening message, he rose to preach, but then became so frightened that he forgot his lesson. He ran out of the building and into the darkness, tripped and fell. Apparently, however, the fall jogged his memory; John came back inside and thrilled the audience with an amazing message—to be sure, a strangely peculiar beginning to a wonderful life's ministry.

Early Years of Preaching

It was 1808 when the local Kentucky Baptists ordained John to preach even without a miraculous call from God. On that same day, he immersed four people. His enthusiasm for preaching knew no limits. He would preach to any crowd, whether in forest groves, cabins, or meeting houses. It has been said that he had a deep, rich voice, and that he spoke with deliberateness. Some in those Cumberland hills said that his voice could be heard for two miles.[5] He loved the Word of God. At noon he would be out in the fields, under a shady tree studying the Scriptures. Then at the evening supper, he would have an open Bible beside his plate, memorizing Scripture.

At age twenty-two, he asked Anne Townsend to share his life in marriage. He had already secured two hundred acres of property, and moved his young bride into a drafty log cabin minus windows or doors. It was not the most exciting place for a honeymoon. The floor was dirt and snow blew in through the cracks between the logs. But it was a challenge that drew them closer together. Slowly they made it into a comfortable home. Within a short time, John Smith acquired more land and money and became a farmer of some ambition. He continued to preach in the Baptist church, and unsurprisingly, what he preached was God's message through the interpretive lens of Calvinism. In the early

1800s, Baptists followed Calvin closely, even more so than today. This included the view that all persons without exception are born into sin. As remedy for this, God had predestined some before they were born to eternal life and the rest to eternal hell. Those numbered among the elect could know about their election by a direct call of the Holy Spirit. Furthermore, if one were blessed enough to be among the chosen, that person could do nothing to fall from the grace of God. Such selective hope was found in John's early preaching.

Reduced to Ashes

Living back in the "holler" of Wayne County, Kentucky, did not provide much chance for temporal success. Realizing this, John sold the Kentucky farm for $1500 and moved to Huntsville, Alabama. Here was an opportunity to purchase 10,000 acres with only small payments to the government. He also came as a Baptist minister. For temporal ambitions, he was doing well, and envisioned himself one day living in a southern mansion with scores of slaves.

That was not to be. One evening, while away from home, lightning struck their log cabin. Anne was visiting a nearby home on a visit of mercy. She was known for her beautiful singing. Hearing that her neighbor was ill, Anne went there, hoping to soothe her neighbor with her songs. She also took her own small infant with her. This left the other small children back at the house under the care of their brothers and sister. John too was away for the day. It was about ten o'clock when Anne heard the screams of horror. She ran outside and saw in the distance her own house on fire. The distance was about half a mile. Immediately she grabbed the infant and ran to the house. Hiram, the oldest boy, met her first, holding the hand of one of the girls. Then she saw three of the other children. Two were still missing! Friends had to restrain her or she would have rushed into the fire to save them. Tragically, the two younger ones, Eli and Elvira, had burned to death.

Two men went and told "Raccoon." He came to the smoldering ashes and tried the best he could to console Anne. It was nearly impossible since his own heart was broken and she could not forgive herself for the unintentional neglect. Raccoon accepted the loss as an act of God and made plans to keep preaching. Anne failed to recover. Within two months, suffering from extreme grief, she became sick and died. Raccoon buried her with the ashes of the two children. He then contracted a fever himself that kept him low for four months. Neighbors thought he would die. For a time he wished he would die, along with his surviving babies who now had to be cared for by a neighbor. It is interesting that local folklore believed that his particular fever could be cured faster if water were withheld. Many times John Smith pleaded for water, but the neighbors, moved as they were, would not give in. One night a neighbor decided to go ahead and give Raccoon his last request, since he was dying anyway. He gave him all the water he could hold. That evening marked the beginning of his cure.

As Raccoon assessed the family tragedy, he was convinced that the Lord had disciplined him for his proud ambitions. He decided to return to southern Kentucky, taking with him hardly anything. He was now thirty-two years old, an ordained Baptist minister of some talent and education. But he had lost his wife and two children. Moreover, he had lost his drive and ambition. He was also profoundly confused over the destiny of his two children. What if they were not of the elect? Would they suffer for all eternity?

Out of the Ashes

Back in Kentucky, a friend invited him to a Baptist Association meeting. In attendance were a large number of ministers and members. He came, wearing unsightly clothes, which included homemade trousers and an old faded coat. If anyone knew him they failed to recognize him. Everyone else ignored him. During the course of the evening, while the leaders of the association went aside to discuss business, two young, inexperienced men were selected to address the hundreds who had gathered outside. At this point someone recognized Raccoon and asked him to speak next after the two men finished. Raccoon, still in depression, was reluctant. The two young men went forward and nervously fumbled around, waiting for the Spirit to supply them something to say. They finally sat down speechless. As people began leaving, something stirred inside Raccoon's own spirit. He walked up to the stand. More began to leave when they saw this one attired so strangely. John cried out to them, "Stay friends, and listen to what the great Augustine said." The exodus paused for a moment. Raccoon informed them how Augustine wished to see three things before he died, "Rome in all her glory. Paul preaching on Mar's Hill. Jesus in the flesh." People were still hesitant to return to their seats. He cried out a second time, "Stay and hear what the great Cato said."[6] He then went on to quote first Cato, followed by Thales, the ancient Greek philosopher. It was suddenly apparent that this crudely dressed gentleman not only had something to say, he knew how to say it. Once he had captured the audience, he gave a stirring message on the redemption of Christ, though with Calvinistic orthodoxy. That evening, some had even climbed into trees to hear this impressive preacher. Raccoon Smith had recovered.

Joining the Campbell Restoration

Yet, his inner spirit still had not achieved tranquility. His Calvinism was confusing as well as unsettling. He preached forcefully, yet his messages even confused himself. On one occasion in March of 1822, he told the sinners in his audience that they should "repent and believe the gospel." He warned, "Jesus died for you; but if you believe not, you must be damned." When he heard what he had just spoken, he knew that it had to sound confusing, even to his own ears. Inwardly, he was thinking, "If the elect who hear me should not believe, then what I am preaching is false, for they are to be saved anyway. And if the non-elect should believe me, my preaching is false, for they are to be lost anyway, since Christ didn't die for them." His honesty and conscience prevented him from continuing. He just told the crowd, "Something is wrong. I am in the dark. We are all in the dark. But how to lead you to the light, or to find the way myself, before God, I know not."[7] He returned home.

By this time he had married Nancy Hurt. It had been a Christmas wedding in 1816. When he entered his home on the evening of that confessional sermon, he was extremely confused as to what to preach, or even if he should preach at all anymore. He and Nancy knelt to pray. He announced to the Lord and to his wife that he would follow only the Bible as his guide and would travel wherever it led him. That pledge initiated his commitment to serious inquiry into Scripture.

He stayed up whole nights at a time weighing Scripture and Calvinism point by point. He was already uneasy with Calvinistic doctrine, especially after his children had died in the flames of the log cabin. He could not bear the thought of his babies passing from a burning cabin into a burning hell. This was the exact place where they would be if they were not of the elect. He searched the Scriptures for better answers. Sometimes he poured over them all night after being in the fields all day. Finally, he concluded that Calvinism rested on the whole structure of the denial of human freedom. Perhaps, he came to believe, those who are "dead in sin" are still free to believe. Perhaps even Christians, who have become "dead to sin," are yet free to sin. Perhaps God's marvelous gift of freedom has been given to all humankind.[8]

This was John Smith's state of mind when someone handed him a copy of the *Christian Baptist*, Alexander Campbell's journal. He was instantly impressed with its scholarship and style. Some of his neighbors in the "holler" had subscribed to the journal for a time, but then canceled their subscription once they realized that Campbell was not a typical Baptist. Smith's own brother had cancelled his subscription. Nevertheless, Smith continued to read it. He declared that he would remain a subscriber; even if Mr. Campbell be the devil himself, he would keep on reading, just because he was impressed with how Campbell said things.

When Alexander Campbell came to Kentucky in the spring of 1824, another local Baptist preacher asked John, "Have you seen brother Campbell yet?" He replied, "No, sir." The friend continued, "Why I have been with him eight days and nights and have heard him every day." This prompted Smith's question, "Is he a Calvinist or an Arminian, an Arian, or Trinitarian?" The preacher answered, "I do not know. He had nothing to do with those things." Smith probed further, "Tell me, does he know anything at all about heart-felt religion?" The preacher responded, "He is one of the most pious, godly men that I was ever in company with in all my life."[9]

Smith then went to hear Campbell himself. The sermon that night was from the text of Paul's letter to the Galatians, chapter 4, the allegory of Hagar and Sarah. Campbell, as was his typical practice, used these two women to distinguish the two covenants. When Campbell had finished the exposition, Raccoon complained to his friend that he did not ride twenty miles to hear a man preach just thirty minutes. The friend said, "Look at your watch." To Smith's surprise, it had been two and a half hours. Raccoon then informed his friend, "Be he saint or sinner, he has thrown more light on that Epistle, and on the whole Scriptures, than I have received in all the sermons that I have ever heard before."[10]

Smith associated more with Campbell, and became persuaded that Campbell was correct in his scriptural interpretation. This association with Campbell's movement continued the rest of his life. For three years following the Stone and Campbell unity meeting of 1832, he rode with John Rogers on horseback to preach unity throughout Kentucky. From 1832 to 1834 there are at least thirty-two reports in the *Millennial Harbinger* detailing stories of their successful journeys.[11] Hundreds were baptized during these travels. Smith also wrote a small pamphlet simply entitled, "Address." Its singular purpose was to encourage Campbell's Disciples to unite with Stone's Christians. Like Campbell, Smith preferred the name "Disciple," but the conviction was not enough to prevent him seeking unity with Stone's "Christians." In a conversation with John T. Johnson, he said:

> Rest assured, you never will, by all your writing, induce anyone who understands the Book, to adopt one of these names to the exclusion of the others; for we know that, after the name *Christian* was given at Antioch, the sacred writers, speaking of the brethren, still call them disciples; and no matter who gave the other name, they were willing to wear it and to suffer under it.[12]

He edited a journal only for a short period. Consequently, history has preserved less of his own thoughts than others in the movement. He did, however, correspond with his second wife, Nancy. In one of his letters to her in 1823 he wrote, "Nancy, I have baptized seven hundred sinners, and capsized fifteen hundred Baptists."[13]

PART TWO: Raccoon's Heart

Nickname and Humor

There are a couple of theories about his nickname, "Raccoon." Probably the most reliable one came from the time when he was at a meeting and introduced himself by saying, "I am John Smith from Stockton Valley, along the south fork of the Cumberland River, down there where they have saltpeter caves and raccoons make their homes."[14] Others said that he often wore a raccoon skin cap. Still others believed he was as crafty as a coon.[15]

"Raccoon" had a great sense of humor. Earlier we noted his prank on the traveling drunken teacher. Smith's parents felt that John's mirthful disposition occasionally led him astray.[16] Some say his natural wit came from his Irish mother. Maybe it was because his life had been marked by periods of tragedy that he needed a little fun to escape it. Frontier life was tough. In late November of 1843 (the "hog-killing season for farmers), Raccoon had gone to Lexington to hear Campbell debate the Presbyterian Nathan Rice. Back home his eight-year-old son had fallen into a vat of scalding water and died before Raccoon returned. Perhaps one of the methods he had learned to cope with the difficult losses and heartaches of frontier life was to seek ways to make life not just tolerable but enjoyable. Nonetheless, his humor endeared him to people.

One time John Smith was walking in the woods. Some boys noticed how strangely he was dressed and started to poke fun at him. "Maybe he is Abraham," said one of them. Another said, "Maybe Isaac." Still another chimed in, laughing, "Is it Jacob?" Raccoon appreciated that the boys learned a few things from Sunday school. So he called out to them, "Boys, I'm neither Abraham, Isaac, nor Jacob; but I am Saul, son of Kish, out looking for his father's jackasses, and I didn't think I would find them so soon!"[17]

John Smith knew Alexander Campbell and appreciated everything he stood for, but could also make fun of him. On one occasion, he described Campbell by saying, "Campbell's nose sat a little bit to the North."[18]

Late in his years, he had a serious discussion with a woman spiritualist. After the discussion, the woman said to him, "Farewell, my brother, I hope to meet you in another world." Raccoon retorted back, "That depends, madam, on which world you are going to, whether I wish to meet you or not."[19]

Integrity and Consistency

John Smith never asked the question, "Is it popular?" He asked, "Is it right?" This was true regardless of who believed or preached it. Someone once told him that if he broke from his Calvinist Baptist church he would go hungry and he would lose his farm. He answered, "Conscience is an article that I have not brought into the market; but if I should offer it for sale, Montgomery County with all its land and houses would not be enough to buy it, much less that farm of 100 acres."[20] His early biographer writes that "his sensitive conscience as a youth prevented him from being involved in the sins of drunkenness, profanity or gambling."[21]

The integrity of his own heart, despite his early theological confusion, was evident to his congregation. He would confess on some points, "I am just as much in the dark as you are." He cared little whether people thought he possessed all the answers or only a few of them.

It was said that nobody could equal the way that Raccoon could preach a point and make it stick. Some say that they remembered his sermons forty or fifty years after they were preached. One story brings together Smith's integrity, consistency, and maybe humor too. He was conducting a gospel meeting in Slate Creek, Kentucky. Across town a Methodist preacher was holding his own meeting. During the week, Smith attended a service by the side of the creek where the Methodist preacher was sprinkling water on a screaming baby. The next day, Raccoon held a baptism by immersion in the same spot. The Methodist preacher was there on the bank with his group. After the ceremony, Smith walked over to the preacher and started to pull him into the creek. The startled preacher asked Smith what he was doing. "I am going to baptize you, sir," Smith replied. The preacher protested, "But I don't want to be baptized." Smith asked, "But don't you believe?" "Certainly I do," said the Methodist preacher. "Then come along, sir," Smith interjected, "Believers must be baptized." "But," the man answered, "I'm not willing to go, and it certainly wouldn't do me any good to be baptized against my will." Raccoon knew he had made his point. He released the man for a second and inquired of him, "Did you not but yesterday baptize a helpless babe against its will? Did you get its consent first?" Smith told the preacher to go his way, and then announced to the crowd that had been mesmerized by the visual display: "Let me know if he ever again baptizes others without their full consent. You yourselves have heard him declare that such a baptism cannot possibly do any good."[22]

Unity of All "Lights"

"Raccoon" Smith was one of the main players in the union between the Campbell and the Stone movements during the 1832 meeting in Georgetown, Kentucky. For some time unity between the two movements had been discussed as a real possibility. Those who attended knew that they had come to discuss the differences, but not debate them. Foremost in their minds was the prayer of Jesus in John 17 where he prayed for the unity of those who came after him. Some of the agenda for the meeting was set, some was not. Many people got up and gave unplanned, spontaneous speeches. It was agreed that one from each party should deliver a main address and in it set forth the scriptural ground of unity as he saw it. The two who were chosen were Barton W. Stone and, in lieu of Alexander Campbell who was unable to attend,[23] "Raccoon" John Smith. Neither had been given advance notice of what the other would say. Stone requested that Smith go first. As has been noted, despite his nickname, John Smith was an eloquent and powerful speaker. One of the early biographers of Smith captured the drama of this highpoint in the Stone-Campbell Movement:

> Smith arose with simple dignity, and stood, prayerful and self-possessed, before the mingling brotherhoods. He felt, as no one else could feel it, the weight of the responsibility that rested on him. A single unscriptural position taken — the least sectarian feeling betrayed — an intemperate word — a proud, unfraternal glance of the eye — might arouse suspicion and prejudice, and blast the hope of union in the very moment when it was budding with so many promises. Every eye turned

> upon him, and every ear leaned to catch the slightest tones of his voice.[24]

Smith spoke of the desirability and practicality of union. He reminded those present of Jesus' prayer for it. But this union, he said, should not be a unity built on human invention, but upon unity with the word of God as the only rule of faith and practice. Opinions could indeed be held freely, but only as opinions. One's opinions are not part of the gospel. Then, speaking for himself, he told them that he was willing to surrender any opinion for the sake of unity. Finally, he summed up his thoughts: "Let us then, my brethren, be no longer Campbellites or Stoneites, New Lights or Old Lights, or any other kind of lights, but let us come to the Bible and to the Bible alone, as the only book in the world that can give us all the light we need."[25]

Next Stone arose and spoke with complete agreement. He then looked at Raccoon Smith and addressed him and the entire audience, "I am willing to give him, now and here, my hand."[26] Both shook hands in fellowship and symbolic union. Hundreds in the audience began to shake hands, many with tears streaming down their faces. Someone started a song and all joined in, "All hail the power of Jesus' name." The following morning was Sunday and everyone broke bread in communion, again a powerful symbol of the unity that had occurred.

For the next three years John Smith would ride with John Rogers, announcing and encouraging unity in every city that had both a Stonite congregation and a Campbellite one. Twelve years later, Smith recalled the event in his short-lived journal *Orthodox Preacher.* He wrote:

> No one ever thought that the Reformers, so-called, had come over to us or that we had gone over to them, but they were required to relinquish their opinions, or we ours. We found ourselves contending for the same great principles of Christianity and we resolved to unite our energies to harmonize the church and to save the world. I entered into it upon

> principle, I think every good has grown out of it, that had it never taken place, our cause in Kentucky would be forever in the rear of the position that it now occupies.[27]

Smith truly believed that unity would never be achieved if people attempted to unify around opinions. He knew all too well that when opinions were made tests of fellowship, walls and divisions quickly followed. He was convinced that the only thing required of any believer was just to believe what the Bible said. Opinions can and should be held, he said, as private property and nothing more. At the 1832 unity meeting, he proclaimed, "Whatever opinions about these and similar objects I may have reached, in the course of my investigations, if I never distract the church of God with them, or seek to impose them on my brethren, they will never do the world any harm."

If the union were to work, he knew that God would have to be behind it. Smith believed strongly in prayer and its efficacy. Even before the unity meetings began, he had been involved in several prayer sessions with Stone and John T. Johnson (from Campbell's side). He continued in prayer afterwards, fervently and constantly. C. J. Conkwright, in a study of the Boone Creek Association of Kentucky, wrote of John Smith, "Elder Smith was a man of extraordinary talents, full of wit and humor, a logician and a warrior. His sermons were generally one and one-half hours long, but when aroused he would preach for two hours or more."[28]

Smith continued to preach for three more decades. Copies exist of two of his last sermons preached in Chillicothe, Missouri at the age of eighty-three. Just before he spoke, Donaldson relates that Smith's favorite hymn was sung. Part of the chorus is as follows:

> There shall friends no more part, nor shall farewells be spoken;
> There'll be balm for the heart that with anguish was broken.
> From afflictions set free, and from God ne'er sever,
> We his glory shall see, and enjoy him forever.[29]

During the singing of the song, "tears flowed copiously down the deeply furrowed cheek of the aged man of God."[30]

Most of John Smith's training had been self taught,[31] yet he was an eloquent and powerful preacher. Alexander Campbell said of him, "Raccoon Smith was the only man I ever saw that a college education could ruin." He went to his reward on February 9, 1868, eighty-four years old, having left an unforgettable mark on the Stone-Campbell fellowship. He told his daughters that he had only one regret in his life—that his sons-in-law were not Christians.

Chapter Five Notes

1. John Augustus Williams, *Life of Elder John Smith* (Cincinnati: R.W. Carroll, 1870), 62.

2. Everett Donaldson, *The Legacy of Raccoon John Smith* (Mt. Sterling, KY.: North Ridge Pub.,1995), 193.

3. Ibid., 55.

4. Williams, *Life of Elder John Smith*, 72.

5. Ibid., 89.

6. Ibid., 114.

7. Ibid., 145.

8. Ibid., 147.

9. Ibid., 163.

10. Ibid., 164.

11. Donaldson, *The Legacy*, 157.

12. Williams, *Life of Elder*, 541-545.

13. Ibid., 258.

14. Leroy Garrett, *The Stone-Campbell Movement: The Story of the American Restoration Movement* (Joplin, Mo.: College Press, 1994), 273-74.

15. P. S. Fall in a note to early biographer, Williams, says the epithet may have originated with Jacob Creath, Sr. On one occasion when Creath was asked to identify Smith, he said, "He is a singe-cat from somewhere among the raccoons." Williams, *Life of Elder John Smith*, 278.

16. Donaldson, *The Legacy*, 41.

17. Recounted in Garrett, *The Stone-Campbell Movement*, 274.

18. Ibid., 278.

19. Willams, *Life of Elder John Smith*, 567-69.

20. Phillips, *A Medley of the Restoration*, 28.

21. Williams, *Life of Elder John Smith*, 38.

22. Ibid., 235-36.

23. Either the distance from Bethany, Virginia, or the time of year (winter) prevented Campbell from attending.

24. Williams, *Life of Elder*, 452.

25. Ibid., 454.

26. Ibid., 455.

27. Quoted in Dickinson, *Cane Ridge Reader*, 343.

28. C. J. Conkwright, *History of the Boone's Creek Association of Kentucky* (Winchester, Ky.: By the author, 1923), 71.

29. Sparks believes that Smith himself had written the words to this song. Elder John Sparks, *Raccoon John Smith: Frontier Kentucky's Most Famous Preacher* (Lexington, Ky.: University of Kentucky Press, 2005), 384.

30. Everett Donaldson, *The Legacy*, 49.

31. The duration of his formal education had been four months.

Chapter Six

JACOB CREATH, JR.

Contender for the Faith

PART ONE: Jacob's Story (1799-1886)

Growing Up Junior

He was called "Junior" to distinguish him from his uncle, Jacob Creath. The suffix was typical of many frontier families. He was the second son born to Lucretia and William on January 17, 1799. Young Jacob had eight brothers and seven sisters, and grew up in a godly home. Father William was a Baptist preacher. His parents must have had special influence, because four of the sons became gospel preachers. When Jacob was a child, Lucretia ran a Sunday school in her home. This was long before this idea caught on in churches. The family always prayed together, and if the father were out of town on one of his preaching trips, Lucretia would make sure the practice continued. Her influence was especially great on Jacob. In later years, Jacob wrote of her that she taught them the Scriptures and gave the family "lessons on morality, modesty, truth, and religion." It was his mother who taught him how to pray, how to study the Bible, and how to worship God.

Philip Donan, who later edited Creath's diary for publication, wrote that Jacob's mother required all the children to memorize the words of beautiful hymns and portions of Scripture.[1]

Seeking Salvation

As he began to mature in years, Jacob faced the question of his own salvation. He had heard enough of his father's sermons to know that he needed saving. Yet, the exact method to obtain it was never made clear, so he spent many candlelit nights searching the Scriptures for some clue on how to be saved. Then, during the day, while the horses were eating, he would read the Bible. He just wanted to be a Christian, but he said that none of the distinguished teachers of his day could give him the desired information on how to become one.[2] One wonders why Jacob's father never supplied the answers. Perhaps his frequent trips away from home left Jacob on his own spiritually. Jacob revealed, "My conscience would sometimes cry out like a frightened child left in the dark by its mother. At times I would try to drown my sorrows and terrors in the vortex of infidelity." His attempts at being an "infidel" brought no satisfaction either.[3] His inherited Calvinism placed all of humanity into two camps: the saved and the damned. Only God truly knew who was in each camp. In fact, after God had placed one in a particular category, nothing could be done to change it. If anyone rebelliously balked at such a view, saying that this arbitration seemed too cruel, the common response would be that all of us because of our depravity deserve to be in the camp predestined for hell. One can only be grateful that God in his rich mercy has decided to save some of us. Therefore, one's life search was to discover into which camp God had predestined her or him. An individual looked for signs, some religious experience, or perhaps a call from God that one could relate to the local church. A vote would then follow which hopefully admitted one into the church. Creath wrote of that time:

> I never saw the day when I did not desire to be good and please God, my maker. I often withdrew to retired places, and prayed to him that I might see a great light shining around me, like Saul of Tarsus; or hear a voice informing me that my sins were pardoned... Under these circumstances, nature sometimes gave way and I went to sleep on my knees, overwhelmed with the dreadful consideration that I was forever lost.[4]

In April of 1817, Jacob attended a meeting of the Meherrin Baptist Association in Brunswick County, Virginia. He was eighteen years old. He traveled some thirty miles from his parents' house and said that he went to this meeting to obtain some "faint hope" of getting any relief from a "great mental agony." The meeting did not afford any. Indeed, he concluded that he could no longer endure such mental agony. Seeing this as his last hope, he asked for the prayers of those assembled. Thereupon, they prayed for him and declared him saved. Creath stated later, "I felt a momentary relief, and the perturbation of mind calmed down; but I was not permanently relieved." At any rate, Jacob's father heard about that "momentary" feeling and announced that his son was now ready to be baptized. Jacob Sr. immersed Jacob Jr. in May, 1817. After the baptism, Jacob felt as never before, declaring, "When I arose out of the water, I experienced the answer of a good conscience towards God. . . . I felt as calm, as tranquil, and as pleasant as a May morning. I had a joy unspeakable and full of glory, a peace with God that is better experienced than expressed."[5] Looking back at the period in which he had sought the answers and struggled throughout his teen years, he said, "Had I been told to believe on the Lord Jesus Christ, repent and be baptized for the remission of my sins, I could have been a Christian at ten years of age, as easily as at seventeen."

Early Sermons

Just one month after his baptism he preached his first sermon. He was barely eighteen years old. The occasion resulted from two young Baptist preachers who had been appointed to preach at his father's church. However, they failed to make the engagement, and so young Jacob gave his own short talk on Galatians 3:10. After the service, an elderly woman politely informed him that while he could word a good prayer, he would never make a preacher.

By 1818, the Baptist church gave Jacob his license to preach. The next year, he attended the University of North Carolina where he studied Latin, Greek, English, and theology. Subsequently in September of 1820, upon the recommendation of his teacher, Jacob was "ordained" as a Baptist minister.

Jacob Creath Jr. served Baptist churches throughout the 1820s. At the same time, he was committed to go where the Word of God might lead him. Recently, he had come across copies of Campbell's *Christian Baptist* and was slowly becoming familiar with Campbell's restoration principles. Definitely affected, Creath began to preach using the "Bible alone," without confessions of faith or creed books. Such behavior did not go unnoticed, and in 1829 the Baptist church tried Creath for heresy. At issue was the operation of the Spirit upon the sinner's heart, whether or not the Spirit could act even before the person had faith. The common idea was that if one was among the elect, God directed his Spirit to move in the selected individual's heart, thereby producing faith. By this time, however, Creath had come to believe that it is God's Word that actually moved people. He was now convinced that the Word of God was the "grand instrument" that changed the hearts of sinners. When the messenger faithfully presented the Savior as Messiah and God's Son, and confronted the sinner with the evidence, then the human mind believed this information as "it believes any other well-sustained proposition, either in morals or mathematics." Creath was convinced that a major part of the conversion process was the proclamation of the gospel as presented in the Word of God. Thus, the mind's acceptance of the correct proposition produced the change in the heart. Moreover, any person possesses that ability and choice to believe. Besides laying out this rational gospel,

Jacob Creath was self-consciously attacking the notion of predestination. Looking back, he penned that the period of the church trial was, in his words, the "most remarkable event of my life." Jacob declared that his analysis of how God changed sinners was truth, and if truth ruined a person, he said, "I'm willing to be ruined by truth."[6]

With such commitment to truth and to the Bible alone, Jacob found himself more and more distant from the Calvinism of his father. Creath, Jr. left the Baptist church and began to associate with the reformers, those trying to restore a simple New Testament Christianity. He had already met Alexander Campbell and a few others, and was greatly impressed by their work and commitment to Scripture. Following the heresy trial, other Baptist associations began to pronounce anathemas on both Jacob Jr. and his uncle, Jacob Sr. The younger Creath declared that he and his uncle were never charged with preaching or teaching anything contrary to Scripture, but the actual charge against them was that they did not receive Baptist traditions or Baptist dogmas as Scripture. From a later perspective he looked back and reflected that there were really three reasons he left the Baptists:

(1) The Baptist sect taught, held, and practiced things which he could not find in the Scriptures.
(2) The Scriptures taught things which the Baptist sect did not teach.
(3) The Baptist sect taught some things which it did not practice.

He said that he finally had to conclude, "It takes more religion to become a Baptist, than it does to go to heaven."

Jacob Creath, Jr. was always controversial. He came into these new ideas in the late 1820s, and quickly started sharing them with other Baptists. It was told that one of his 1827 sermons in Mississippi almost caused a civil insurrection. A local camp meeting burned his image in effigy. He believed for awhile that his life was in serious danger. A certain Dr. Line told Creath that had it not been for the constitution and the laws of the country, Creath would have been hung twenty times. To be sure, it was not only Baptists who found Creath no longer to their liking, but Methodists, Presbyterians, and a number of Episcopalians had encountered Creath and disliked him.

Publisher and Preacher

Creath knew that he needed a public vehicle to explain his views. So, in 1830, based in Lexington, Kentucky, Creath inaugurated his monthly paper, the *Christian Examiner.* Its main intention was to be a defense of his beliefs. He also used the paper to rebut a pamphlet being circulated by John Taylor, a Baptist preacher out of Franklin County, Kentucky, that had been written to expose the errors of "Campbellism." Besides publishing and writing, Creath traveled widely, preaching across Tennessee, Kentucky, South Carolina, Alabama, and Mississippi.

In September of 1831, he fell deeply in love with and married a young widow, Susan Bedford. He said of her: "She was a pure-hearted, noble-minded woman; neat, industrious, and economical; a good wife, a loving mother, an indulgent mistress."[7] She was a great helper to his life for seven years and, it seems, a reason to reduce some of his frenetic activity. He had moved to a farm formerly owned by his great uncle just outside of Lexington, Kentucky. So he would farm during the week and then preach on Saturday and Sunday at adjacent counties. The years 1832 and 1833 were especially productive years. He wrote of them: "I immersed a great many persons in the years 1832-33. In one case we cut very thick ice and immersed when the snow was deep on the ground."

Jacob held a debate in 1834 with William Green, a professor of ancient languages. Green, a Presbyterian, had issued a challenge that he would debate anyone who would defend "Campbellism." Creath accepted the challenge, though with reluctance. He said that he really preferred to stay out of such controversy, and did not want to start a war with Presbyterians. The debate was held, and in his own thinking, he believed he had clearly beaten Green.

The following year, he engaged in several preaching tours. One was a ten-day meeting held in Versailles, Kentucky. Creath shared the experience with John T. Johnson. Jacob would preach and then Johnson would do the exhorting. It turned out to be a great meeting. A hundred and forty responded and were baptized. Creath loved the experience and wrote later, "I never attended such a meeting before or since, nor do I ever expect to attend another such a one this side of heaven. I was never so happy at any other meeting in my life."[8] The following three years, Creath participated in more successful evangelistic campaigns across Kentucky.

Life changed suddenly in 1838 when Susan was thrown while riding a horse. The extent of her injuries was never known. All that is known was that she never recovered from it. Subsequently, Creath remained at home more and assisted in the rearing of the children who were still small. Yet, Susan's health showed no improvement, and many thought she would die. For that reason, Jacob and Susan decided to move to Missouri. Susan's family already lived there, and she expressed her desire to die at her father's house, surrounded by her brothers and sisters. Additionally, Jacob thought that the move would improve his "worldly condition,"[9] and maybe provide him greater influence in his ministry. So, in the fall of 1839, the Creaths made the six hundred mile move to Missouri. They arrived in Monticello, Missouri by early 1840. Susan failed to improve and her physician confined her most of the time to her bed. In the following year (July, 1841) Susan died of "pulmonary consumption."[10]

In October, Jacob moved to Palmyra, Missouri. By the next year (1842) he had married Prudence Rogers and the marriage continued until his death. They had become acquainted during one of his preaching trips to Paducah, Kentucky. Jacob referred to her as a "precious jewel." She proved a great benefit in raising his children from his first wife. Together, he and Susan had five children in all, one of which was his stepson, Sydney, from Susan's former marriage.

The 1840s were especially successful and productive years. Creath preached his way across Missouri, up into Iowa and Indiana, holding gospel meetings and planting churches. Under his guidance the church in Shelbyville, Missouri grew from nine members to over two hundred. The next decade saw him preaching not only in his home state, Missouri, but participating in meetings in Illinois, Indiana, Ohio, West Virginia, and one occasion even before the Missouri legislature. At one spot in Clinton, Mississippi, three drunken rowdies assaulted him while he was preaching and almost killed him.

One of his interests in the later 1850s was in the need for Bible revision. He was convinced that a more accurate version of the Bible would help to counteract errors in the text of the Common Version as well as various denominational errors. He believed that Campbell's translation, *Living Oracles*, was a wonderful step forward. In it Campbell had translated the Greek word *baptizo* into English as "immerse" and not merely transliterated it as "baptize." Such a brave move on Campbell's part, he felt, would surely bring an end to one of the heresies of his time.

Twilight Years

Jacob Creath called the years 1861-65 the "most difficult part" of his life. Among its many tragedies, the Civil War left him bitter. In the opening two years of the war, his own home had been searched by Federal soldiers on six occasions. Creath wrote about the war: "I must therefore do one of two things. I must first omit it entirely, or I must make a faithful record of what was done to me by the Federal soldiers and to my family." In his diary he stated, "During the 4 or 5 years of the war I was compelled to remain at home to take care of my family, and could not go from home, as before the war, to preach."[11] At the war's height, he had even received a colonel's commission audaciously requesting him to raise a company of men. Jacob declined. He let it be known that he could not be induced by honors nor by money to go to war.

In 1863, he got up to preach and found a letter addressed to him lying on his Bible. It had been signed by "A Union man." Creath read the letter publicly. In it the writer had asked why Creath never prayed for the President of the United States. Creath answered that he was opposed to introducing politics into the pulpit. He then gave anyone in the audience a chance to speak up if they chose and make some reply. No one did. But Jacob was not finished with the matter. He went on and prayed "that the President of the United States might administer the Constitution as all his predecessors in office had done, from the foundation of the Government up to the time he came into office, and that God would grant him repentance for all his sins, and forgive him for all the evils he had brought on this nation." Creath wrote of this occasion, "I was not arrested."[12]

Following the cessation of the war, Creath returned to more extended preaching tours. Throughout the remainder of the 1860s, he preached as far east as North Carolina and Virginia, his birth state. In his diary of 1871, he wrote, "I am now in the 55th year of my ministry, of which I must shortly give an account. Two things grieve me. First, that I have done so little good; second that I have done so many wrong things."[13] His age was slowly catching up with him. He made only a few preaching trips during the last fifteen years of his life.

Jacob Creath had preached to one group for nearly forty years, the congregation at Palmyra, Missouri. They affectionately referred to him there as "Father Creath." He was now an old man, but still had a passion for the message. Creath was seventy-nine years old when in 1877 someone heard him and said that he could still preach with "great power" and that, even though his physical frame was wearing out, his mental faculties knew no failure.[14] One author wrote of him, "Our fathers all seem to wear out in old age, but not so with Jacob Creath."

Early in 1884, the editor of the famed journal, *American Christian Review*, stopped by Creath's home to visit him. The editor wrote that Creath was indeed feeble in body (he had become by this time quite deaf), but also noted that he was still fully possessed of all his mental powers. The editor, John Rowe, wrote, "Of course it was a great pleasure to me to grasp the hand, and to look into the bright and piercing eyes of one of the great pioneer preachers of the 'Far West'—one of the great campaigners of our cause in the great state of Missouri."

Jacob Creath, Jr. died of sudden illness in January 8, 1886. His phenomenal preaching career had been long in years and wide in geography. Innumerable hundreds were brought to the Lord through his ministry. For many who were trying to restore simple New Testament Christianity, like those among the Stone-Campbell movement, he had become a household name. David Lipscomb wrote of his death, "We presume there are none now whose labors were so active, and extended over so large a field, as was brother Creath's."[15]

PART TWO: Jacob's Heart

John Rowe described Jacob Creath this way:

> He is six feet in height, has a long and high head, a sharp and aquiline nose, very penetrating blue-gray eyes, a firmly set mouth, and a deep sonorous voice—all these traits denoting great energy of character and intellectual force, and reminding us very much of the characteristics of Alexander Campbell, whom, in his general contour, he resembles.[16]

A Sober Look at Life

Of all the reformers covered so far, perhaps Creath had the most serious disposition. He himself wrote, "From childhood I was of a serious, contemplative disposition, deriving more pleasure from association with the aged than with the young, and gay, and frivolous."[17] Others knew him as a moody person. One early biographer, said that Jacob's face often looked sour. One wonders if some of his sober character came from the conditions in which he was working and living. For two years (1833/34) a huge cholera outbreak devastated the region in and around Lexington. Statistics showed that anywhere from five to seven hundred people died during this epidemic. Creath's own family caught the disease, but managed to survive it. Jacob knew at least forty people who died within sight of his farm. He wrote that he became the physician for his family. "We could not obtain doctors from town. It resembled more what I suppose the Day of Judgment will be, than any time I have ever witnessed in this world."

Yet he was not completely humorless. Rogers stated that at times Jacob could find humor in things; yet at other moments he could be exceedingly sad.[18] Upon hearing of his death David Lipscomb wrote that Jacob had a temper that sometimes was hard to control and often possessed great irritability.[19] Though he could sometimes be abrupt in his dealing with others, those who knew Jacob well believed that he never meant ill treatment toward anyone. As one explanation of Creath's gruffness, Rogers stated that Creath never had a "fine trainer of manners and couth in his early years with which some have been blessed."[20]

Inside the Building

Creath believed that houses of worship should be respectable places, where worship to one's God is done with utter solemnity. In his writings, one discovers several injunctions regarding what happens as Christians enter to worship. First, he felt that people should always be punctual, so as not to disturb others who are listening to the speaker or to the Scriptures being publicly read. People should leave all laughter and joking outside, as they remember the One they have come to worship.[21] Furthermore:

> There should be no talking or laughing or whispering, as though we had come there for chit-chat, and to hear and report all the news of the week past, and like we had met in a ball-room or theater, instead of a place of worship. . . . One reason why we hear so many complaints of the preachers is that the people are not in a proper frame of mind to hear; they come thoughtless, prayerless, without reflection and meditation. . . . No wonder, then, they return as they came, without benefit, full of levity and frolic, as if they had been to a circus or a horse-race.[22]

Dogs should be left at home.

> No well-bred persons will carry their dogs to places of worship. Even the heathen would not allow dogs to enter their temples. There are two ways to prevent them from following you. Shut them up or kill them. . . . I have seen congregations or the worship destroyed by dogs. Almost every person thinks his pet dog can follow him to meeting, and if every pet dog goes to meeting, then it will be a meeting of dogs.[23]

Other things of this world should also be left at the door. He considered it rude to carry one's cigar or pipe near a place of worship, and even ruder to stand at the door or inside and puff on them. Such people he felt should be marked as "rowdy." All attention should be focused on the cause for the gathering. Therefore, he remarked, "No orderly person will whittle sticks or pare his nails with his knife during the hours of worship; nor chew tobacco, nor spit the juice on the floor, or walls, or pulpit; nor stand in the aisles or doors to prevent passing, nor sleep during preaching."[24]

A Bold Proclaimer of Truth

Creath found enemies nearly everywhere he went. Even within his own movement, there were many who disagreed with him. Creath was outspoken against the use of instrumental music and the missionary society, and he spoke loudly, not just with his voice, but also with his pen. He wrote for his own publication, *The Christian Examiner*, and also for the *American Christian Review*, *Bible Advocate*, and *Christian Pioneer*. In total, he wrote more than four hundred essays addressing the religious questions of his day.

Creath stood boldly for all his convictions, thoroughly convinced that his position was closest to the truth. Of all the early critics of instrumental music in worship, his voice was the most outspoken. He wanted no one to doubt his stance on the issue and that he was "thoroughly anti-organ." One author said, "Like a lion devours its prey, Creath sought to devour the enemies of truth." Indeed, he so adamantly stood for truth that some thought he was egotistical or perhaps had an exaggerated feeling of his own importance. One of Earl West's articles about him was called simply "Iron Duke."[25] A younger contemporary said that Creath opposed nothing mildly that he considered false.[26] It was said that he never trimmed his sails to go with the popular breeze and never apologized for any truth contained in the Old or New Testaments.[27]

As Creath brought his autobiography to a close, he commented, "I have said what I believed. I have learned from God's Word, and what I thought would lead to unite the minds of our brethren in the pursuit of truth. And I have endeavored to speak in such a manner, that for those very persons with whom I was unable to agree in all things, I could, nevertheless, most sincerely declare my regard and veneration."

He held firm opinions against the missionary society which was gaining acceptance in the young movement. He believed that a person could take the gospel on his own. Missionaries could benefit from the help of individual churches without having to depend upon an organized association that would train and send out its preachers. He felt that Scripture spoke of no higher organization than the church. The new society was a human plan that violated the divine one. He was particularly upset that Campbell had given his support to the society, especially since he knew that Campbell had formerly opposed it. He had known Campbell since the 1820s and 30s (especially in Campbell's more conservative *Christian Baptist* days). So Creath wrote to Campbell and said, "If you were right in the *Christian Baptist*, you are wrong now. If you are right now, you were wrong then." Creath's advocacy of allowing the church alone to send out its missionaries was so strong that he said: "When I am dead, I should like for it to be engraved upon my tombstone —'Here lies Jacob Creath, who opposed all Societies to spread the Gospel except the individual churches of Jesus Christ, because he believed such Societies to be destructive of the liberty of the churches and mankind."

It was clear that Jacob had great respect and admiration for his father. When later he assembled a biographical sketch of his father, he included some of his father's personal letters and other correspondence. Creath concluded:

> If they [the letters] do not breathe the spirit of a New Testament Christian, then I am no judge of such a spirit. Independently of his being my father, I can say that I have never known a man who more sincerely and ardently loved God, his Word, his Kingdom, and his people, than he did. He had his faults and his sins, like other men, but a more ardent and zealous man I never saw.

That tremendous respect for his father as a Baptist minister made it all the more difficult throughout his life to determine just who was a "Christian" and who was not. In 1850 he wrote to Campbell about people in denominations who were trying to lead godly lives the best they knew how. He stated that many have been sprinkled, believing it was valid baptism. Furthermore, their conviction about it is as strong as ours that only immersion is New Testament baptism. He said they have been mistakenly taught by their parents and their preachers, and most of them do not have the time to examine the subject for themselves and find out which act God commanded. He wrote that these people really want to be "altogether Christians," and "they are as good Christians as ourselves, except, perhaps, in baptism and in the frequent celebration of the supper." He realized also that these people have great hearts. He stated, "Many of them excel our people in other parts of piety—in practical duties. I believe the people are honestly mistaken—not intentionally disobedient to God—but simply mistaken in what constitutes obedience or baptism." Nonetheless, Creath knew that these people needed further instruction, and that those who deluded them needed the truth unashamedly proclaimed to them. Perhaps this was why some remembered that in his preaching he always chose his words carefully, yet with total conviction and deliberateness. He would speak to edify, but when aroused some said he became a lion.

A Spiritual View of Life

Jacob was deeply concerned that his family be reared in a spiritual atmosphere. Certainly family worship helped in his ambition. He described it this way:

> We have been in the habit, as a family, ever since we have existed as such, of worshipping our Creator morning and evening, by reading his Word, and offering to him the incense of prayer and thanksgiving and praise. When my children became old enough, each of us read a verse in rotation, until we had finished the lesson of the hour. When I was from my home, my wife acted as the priestess of the family in presenting their spiritual sacrifices to Jehovah. We read the Bible through in course, and had completed that delightful series of lessons ten times while my children were with me. . . . In the dark hours of affliction and sorrow we worshiped God, as a family, three times a day.[28]

Apparently that atmosphere produced results. Creath wrote later, "All the persons who ever were members of my household for more than a year, with one or two exceptions, professed conversion." Furthermore, he viewed his own time spent in devotion to God as of supreme importance. In his autobiography, in a line penned in 1862, he stated, "How few of what may be called happy days does any person enjoy in this world unless they are spent in devotion, prayer and praise."[29]

Convinced of his obligation to help the younger generation while he was still here, Creath shared more details of his daily family practices:

> I rise at four o'clock in the morning in the summer, and at five in the winter time. . . . My wife then rises and dresses herself, and we read a chapter in the Bible—I one in the morning , and she one in the evening. We then unite in prayer to God for his blessing and direction. . . . After breakfast, I walk about one mile west of my house, to a woods, and there I spend fifteen to twenty minutes in private prayer, where I have more real happiness in close communion with God than all this world can afford me. I would not be deprived of this source of enjoyment for this world and all its vanities.[30]

Creath's commitment to the Word of God was uncommonly strong. Throughout the course of his life, he read the Bible cover to cover more than fifty times. His practice was to begin in Genesis on the first day of the year and finish with Revelation on December 31. David Lipscomb knew Creath above all else as a man of prayer, one who studied his Bible faithfully and constantly until his death. It was said of Creath that he "loved the truth, pure and unadulterated—truth unmixed with human tradition or human speculation. God's Holy Word was to him all and in all." William Rogers says that Creath would "sooner by far lose the last drop of his blood than part with this blessed Book of books, with its glorious and precious promises." Another contemporary wrote that Creath was a man who knew the Lord and his Word so intimately that the "very presence of Creath was a sermon and his prayers poured forth as from a fountain of devotion."

William Rogers was with Jacob Creath one weekend in the late 1850s while they were staying at a Christian sister's place. They had shared a meal together, talked for a few hours, read the Word, and prayed until it was time to retire for the evening. Rogers related that about midnight he heard a moaning sound coming from Creath's room. He concluded that Creath had apparently eaten too much for supper. The next morning while they were sharing breakfast, Rogers noticed that Creath seemed especially depressed and unusually quiet. After a few minutes Jacob walked over and whispered to Rogers, "Will you walk with me? I am greatly burdened by sorrow." The two men walked together outside for awhile, entered a forest, and came to a little stream. There was a beautiful grove of cedars nearby and birds were flying overhead. The morning sun sent its rays down through the leaves of the trees. Creath stood motionless, perhaps taking it all in. Then he turned to his friend Rogers and said, "Come, let us pray." So both men on the spot moved to their knees. Jacob began to pray out loud. Rogers said that he never remembered ever hearing such a prayer. The prayer was remorseful and replete with self-acknowledged helplessness. Jacob's voice was trembling and he wept bitterly. He pleaded with the Lord for help and forgiveness. Rogers wrote, "Such a prayer I may possibly have heard before or since, but of this I have no recollection.[31]" Jacob finished and wiped his cheeks, wet with tears. He then requested Rogers to pray. Rogers recalled that he did the best he could, asking the God of all comfort for help. He prayed for Creath and his health, as well as for Creath's family, separated by hundreds of miles. That was the extent of his memory. Then Rogers added, "I have understood from many brethren that they, too, have passed through similar touching scenes with this brother."[32]

Jacob Creath, Jr. also had a sharper side. He possessed no patience for anyone or any preacher who speculated or theorized what was not revealed in Scripture. In a written request about how a sinner is born again, his response was adamant: "The word of God is the grand instrumentality by which the hearts of sinners are changed; and that when the evidence of our Savior's Messiahship or Divinity is fully set forth, the human mind finds no difficulty in believing it, as it believes any other well-sustained proposition, either in morals or mathematics."[33] He concluded his argument: "And if something has to be added to this evidence, beyond our own resources, before we can believe and obey, we are nearly in the condition that we would have been in if God had not spoken to us at all."[34]

Creath was not shy to go on the attack, and not always with restrained anger. It is possibly this rougher exterior that led Richard Hughes to dismiss Creath as a "cantankerous" old Kentuckian.[35] Yet such a pejorative adjective oversimplifies the man and his contributions. David Lipscomb wrote of him, "His writings were noted chiefly for their robustness, vigor and force. But in his preaching he was frequently as simple as a child, as tender and gentle as a woman. . . . I have heard but few preachers that could present the gospel with more simplicity, tenderness and love than Brother Creath."

Creath preached for sixty-six years and made a major impact on the Stone-Campbell movement. He left us with a memory of a unique, colorful character. Two years prior to his death he wrote his own obituary. He believed that since Jesus and the apostles all died without a funeral sermon being preached for them, he did not need one either. He only requested that he be buried in a cheap, plain coffin with his pocket Bible placed under his head and a copy of Campbell's translation of the Scriptures beneath that.

Chapter Six Notes

1. Philip Donan, *Memoirs of Jacob Creath, Jr.* (Cincinnati: Chase & Hall, 1877), 45

2. Ibid., 48.

3. Ibid.

4. Ibid., 49.

5. Ibid., 54.

6. John T. Johnson was a member of the Baptist church that tried Creath, as well as being present at the trial itself. Later, Johnson would join the Stone-Campbell movement and would go on to baptize thousands across the South. Johnson told Creath in 1852 that had it not been for Creath, he would never have become part of the Reformation.

7. Donan, *Memoirs of Jacob Creath,* 133.

8. Ibid., 104.

9. Ibid., 108.

10. One form of tuberculosis.

11. Donan, 182.

12. Ibid., 195.

13. Ibid., 206.

14. John A. Brooks, "Jacob Creath," *Gospel Advocate* 19, no. 5 (February 1, 1877): 67.

15. David Lipscomb, "Death of Jacob Creath," *Gospel Advocate* 28, no. 3 (January 20, 1886): 38.

16. Others had said also that Creath's "person and carriage" made them think of Campbell. John A. Brooks, "Jacob Creath," *Gospel Advocate* 19, no. 5 (February 1, 1877): 67. It is interesting that Creath wore a hairpiece to cover his bald head.

17. Donan, *Memoirs of Jacob Creath,* 57.

18. William C. Rogers, *Recollections of Men of Faith* (Rosemead, Calif.: Old Paths Book Club, 1960): 243ff.

19. David Lipscomb, "Death of Jacob Creath," *Gospel Advocate* 28, no. 3 (January 20, 1860): 38.

20. Rogers, *Recollections*, 237.

21. Donan, *Memoirs of Jacob*, 184.

22. Ibid., 185.

23. Ibid., 187.

24. Ibid.

25. Earl West, "The 'Iron Duke,'" included in reprint of Philip Donan, *Memoirs of Jacob Creath, Jr.* (Indianapolis: Religious Book Service, n.d.). The title comes from the occasion of John F. Rowe, editor of *American Christian Review,* upon hearing of Creath's death, nicknamed him "The Iron Duke." Rowe compared him to the Duke of Wellington, saying that throughout Creath's life he could neither be bought nor sold. West, 16.

26. Rogers, *Recollections*, 234.

27. Ibid., 236.

28. Donan, *Memoirs of Jacob*, 105-106.

29. Ibid., 188.

30. Ibid., 189.
31. Rogers, *Recollections*, 248.
32. Ibid.
33. Donan, *Memoirs of Jacob*, 80.
34. Ibid.
35. Richard Hughes, *Reviving the Ancient Faith: The Story of the Churches of Christ in America* (1996; 2nd edition, Abilene, Tex.: Abilene Christian University Press, 2008), 41.

Chapter Seven

THE BALANCE OF HEAD AND HEART

Historians are a strange people. Their business is that of collection and recitation. At the same time, this business is a selective enterprise. As historians rifle through the mountains of data behind them, they decide what is worthy of passing to the next generation. They have no other choice. To tell the complete history of the past two hundred years would take approximately two hundred years. So, these unique people must decide what is worthy of preservation. They selectively tell only the part of history that assists in the understanding of a movement or of one's family or one's self. Sometimes the selection is based on the question of what material will better prepare one for the future. Each historian seeks to retrieve from history that which answers his or her own questions.

For a long time historians in Churches of Christ have sought mainly information about the leaders from the nineteenth century for the purpose of solidifying a body of doctrine. The debates of Alexander Campbell and others, therefore, have proved especially helpful as those in later centuries sought to defend their own stances on what was seen as central issues of the faith. Usually the central issues to Churches of Christ have been the doctrines that set them apart from other groups.

Even redemption has been seen mostly in terms of legal standing and saving purity, despite the fact that so much of the New Testament envisions salvation as relational,[1] first with the Lord and then with other brothers and sisters in the faith. No wonder then these Stone-Campbell leaders from earlier generations reappeared in later times as one or two-dimensional characters only. To use the terms from the research of Sperry into left-brain/right-brain,[2] the re-tellers of early stories focused much more on "left-brain" activity. These early leaders were the bearers of correct information, of "sound doctrine." Their inner selves, i.e. their "hearts," with all of its accompanying feeling, sensitivity, artistry, creativity, and humor have usually been overlooked. Also hindering this process of re-discovery is the fact that these preachers like Campbell, Stone, Scott, and others have been known mostly through what they said, wrote, and published, and not so much through what they did or felt. To be sure, what they said was of utmost importance. Then, as the chronological distance increased, these figures slowly morphed into teachers only. Indeed, one cannot imagine sitting down to table with them, or swapping a funny story, or weeping with them at what a movement has become.

As has been shown, Alexander Campbell was a man of tremendous intellect, yet possessed a heart large enough to include the families from two marriages as well as compassion for a dynamic movement. Even those who debated him fiercely in public forums noticed his kindness and genuine respect for them as individuals. Some of them became life-long friends. His home was open to them at any time, just as it was for the students from his college at Bethany. He entertained countless students in his home, feeding as well as lodging them. Alexander desired his own children to know the Bible with all of its facts, as well as knowing the Bible's divine Author. He believed that one's relationship with the Lord and time spent with him were vital to the spiritual life.

Music could fuel the soul, and Campbell provided the movement with hymnals for congregational and family singing. Like Barton

Stone, he cringed when he entered houses of worship where members sat apathetic in prayer. Human physical bodies, not only minds and lips, should be involved in worship. Thus, both Stone and Campbell advocated kneeling or standing whenever possible during prayer. One's spiritual attitude was reflected in how one's body was positioned.

In an article called, "Short Sermon on Christian Practice," Campbell emphatically brought the heart with its emotions back to the Christian lifestyle. He wrote:

> But what is holiness? It is sanctification. And what is sanctification? It is a separation, or consecration to God in heart as well as in state. And what is this separation of heart, but conformity of views, feelings, and desires; or an approving and choosing the same thing? To will what God wills, to love what he loves, and to hate what he hates, is holiness in principle and in heart, and to carry this out in practice is holiness in fact and in truth.[3]

Campbell's position on empirical knowledge and his opposition to revival enthusiasm and abuses is well known. Less known is that Campbell did not preclude all spiritual phenomena. At least twice he believed that he had had premonitions of disaster. Once was during the shipwreck on his way to America and the other was while he was in Great Britain. Something at the time made him feel that a terrible event had occurred back home. Indeed it had. His beloved son, Wycliffe, drowned while Campbell was away.[4]

Furthermore, Alexander Campbell knew that any real success in this life came after spending much time on one's knees away from the crowds. One's personal closet was the best location for the most sincere communication with the Lord. God was truly present in those times, and if one listened, as well as spoke, he could discern more of the inexplicable reality of God. Campbell felt that prayer was a time of self-examination into all of one's personal ambitions and goals. A person should withhold nothing from the throne of heaven, but bring to God all heartaches, sins, and shortcomings. Only time spent with the Creator of the universe could shape one into the image of the Creator's Son.

Campbell's heart was broken and molded by losses—of his wife, Margaret, later his parents, and even his children who died prematurely. In later years, Campbell traveled less frequently. This was not only due to health but to his desire to remain closer to the ones he loved. Campbell loved his family passionately and reveled in the moments when, as a family, all the Campbells could share in Bible study and devotionals.

Walter Scott can perhaps be credited with the inauguration of the five-step plan of evangelism, which he used so effectively on the Western Reserve with children and their families. However, Scott knew that the gospel ran through deeper waters and rested on the proclamation of Jesus Christ as the Son of God. He wrote in 1844:

> Although this was the actual and practical restoration of the central truth in our religion to its proper place in the Christian system, many failed nevertheless to see it, and were carried away wholly by the easier and more popular generalization of faith, repentance, baptism, etc. till, in fact, they do not know their own principles when they are advocated.[5]

These waters were not devoid of heart-felt devotion. Scott declared in 1835, "A cold medium must be exceedingly offensive to Jesus Christ."[6]

Each of these leaders discussed in this book had a great love for people. Even "cantankerous" Jacob Creath, Jr. wept over those who were not in the Lord's kingdom. Co-workers such as William Rogers remembered Creath's trembling voice and audible weeping as the latter prayed. Rogers also commented that several, in fact, had witnessed these visible expressions of emotion from Creath. Samuel Rogers, John's older preaching brother, bemoaned the fact that, while they had done away with the mourner's bench, they had also eliminated mourners.[7] In Kentucky,

Barton Stone had possessed slaves, but after his move north he released them.[8] Yet, he never let them wander too far from his memory. Part of his homecoming to Kentucky in 1838 was a chance for a reunion with them. They too were his family. Many in the reunited circle wept as Stone prayed spiritual blessings for their temporal as well as spiritual welfare.

"Raccoon" John Smith had hoped to remain on the fringe of ministry after the loss of two of his children. However, when many people began to exit the hall where a Baptist association meeting was being held, perhaps bored or disappointed, Smith literally rose to the occasion and addressed the group, begging them to stay. His great affection for people kept him from being an unproductive spectator on the edge of the movement. Indeed, he was drawn back to the center of it and remained there until he died.

Barton Stone's heart ached when, in later years, he noticed the movement's quest for unity among all believers veer off in another direction. He was deeply saddened to see how self-righteous pride replaced humility and love for the lost. Many of Stone's final published messages were pleas for ministers to return to brotherly love. He felt that those who always sought to win arguments and never submit on a single point should spend more time in devotion to God. Drawing close to the throne of God will create proper attitudes and especially humility. Leonard Allen informs the modern disciple that as these historic controversies heightened and debates continued to be aggressively pursued, Robert Richardson, following in the steps of Stone, attempted to bring people back to the things of the Spirit and the devotional life.[9] Newell Williams' recent biography of Stone attributes Stone's theology, as well as his social and religious practice, all to his Presbyterian upbringing. Williams claims that this spirituality always "worshiped a God of love and grace revealed in the gospel of Jesus Christ, maintained a chastened view of human nature and identified the knowledge, enjoyment and service of God as the purpose of life."[10] Stone responded to the love of God with his whole life; assembling at worship was a joy and never a duty. He was distressed that in some places he had witnessed church members attending to the Lord's Supper "as a duty, or as a custom, and not as a divine privilege—many of them sitting and gazing around on the multitude, and passing events around them, while they were receiving the symbols of the body and blood of Christ!"[11]

Many of John Rogers' sermons focused on the grace and love of God. He related that his own heart was full of love for God, his church, and the world. Witnessing schisms among Christians with a world still in darkness broke his heart. This was one reason he was convinced that the occupation of preaching was not a method to scare people away from hell, but rather a means of helping individuals understand their own hearts.

History has repeatedly given shape to people's lives in large pendulum swings. One age reacts to the beliefs of a previous period. Then the next age responds in kind. The problem historically has been in overreaction. In the later nineteenth century, those fearful of rampant and wild emotion in the frontier revivals retreated to a more restrictive and regimented religion. They desired a religion that could be both tamed and contain certain truth. Berryhill notices that Campbell's model was designed to avoid the abuses so prevalent among the revivals, yet it also spawned a "dominance of reason over feeling, expository lectures, and intensive Bible study among the Disciples."[12] Books and journals were published and circulated. Debates were held and won. By the twentieth century, fewer and fewer actively thought about the place of the heart. This oversight was by no means intentional, but the belief was there that if the head were aligned properly one need not worry much about the heart. It would surely follow. The only problem was that it did not. In Andrew Wall's recent survey of those who have left Churches of Christ (based on a sampling from southern California), 77% of respondents reported being drawn to a church with a more heartfelt/expressive style of worship; 73% reported that the "worship service was uninspiring."[13]

As the twenty-first century progresses, it will be wise for those who seek more balance in their spiritual lives to occasionally look behind, and perhaps even acknowledge that Christianity is both a "left" and "right" brained religion. Early Stone-Campbell movement leaders, as has been shown, allowed for both sides of the brain to be controlled by the Christ. Some forty years after the movement's inception, Moses Lard wrote that those who take part in discussions about restoration of the first-century church "are frequently accused of believing in and having only a religion of the head." He continued, "It was the high theoretic ground assumed by our brethren that caused their practice to appear unduly defective." Lard, aware of the deficiency, argued for a reformation of practice. He stated: "What is respectable is not enough. We should, in our conduct, as a people, exhibit a sublime moral spectacle to the world. Our faith should be clear and strong; our piety deep and pure; our love intense and large; our devotion to God cordial and uniform, and our practice a simple and faultless conformity to the will of Christ."[14] Stated another way, he urged his brothers and sisters to exhibit a faith that encompasses clearly one's whole being as held captive by Jesus Christ.

In a moving autobiographical essay, Richard Hughes shares how he came to view the early restoration leaders as real flesh and blood persons of God. He reflects:

> On many days, I read the written witness these men had left behind and found myself stunned, simply unable to read further. On many days, my reading of these texts was as much a devotional exercise as anything else, for I found myself edified beyond measure by Barton Stone, Tolbert Fanning, David Lipscomb, James A. Harding, R. H. Boll, J. W. Armstrong, and a host of others just like them.[15]

By dipping once again into history one can hear the words of Walter Scott, accompanying a fellow preacher on the way to a gospel meeting. Laying out the plans for the evening, Walter turns to his friend and urges, "I will speak first, and I will strike at the head. Then it will be your turn. You strike the heart."

Chapter Seven Notes

1. For example, Paul speaks of being buried in baptism into "union with" Christ Jesus (Romans 6:3-5), and everyone who is baptized into Christ has "put on" Christ (Galatians 3:26-27).

2. See p. 20 in this text.

3. Alexander Campbell, "Short Sermons on Christian Practice—No. IV. On Bible Reading—No. 1," *Millennial Harbinger* 2nd series, no. 3 (1839): 343. See also Robert Rea, "'Holiness' in the Writings of Early Stone-Campbell Movement Leaders," *Stone Campbell Journal*, 8.2 (Fall, 2005): 163-180.

4. Thomas H. Olbricht, "The Holy Spirit in the Early Restoration Movement," *Stone Campbell Journal* 7:1 (2004): 19.

5. Scott, *Protestant Unionist* 1 (25 September, 1844): 292.

6. *The Evangelist* 4 (September, 1835): 205.

7. Samuel Rogers, *Autobiography of Samuel Rogers* (Cincinnati: Standard Publishing, 1909), 30.

8. Hughes contends that it was Stone's countercultural move of emancipating his slaves as well as his gospel preaching that brought about the massive emancipation of slaves that occurred among Churches of Christ in the very first decade of the nineteenth century. Before Stone, very few in the South had even thought of freeing their slaves at that early date. Richard T. Hughes, "How Barton Stone Led Me to Christ Anew: An Autobiographical Essay," *Stone Campbell Journal,* 11.2 (Fall, 2008): 174. Williams believes that it may have been Stone's disappointment with the United States government's failure to emancipate slaves that led to his advice for Christians not to participate in government. Williams, *Barton Stone*, 231.

9. Robert Richardson, *Communings in the Sanctuary*, ed. C. Leonard Allen (Abilene, Tex.: Leafwood Publishers, 2000).

10. Williams, *Barton Stone*, 6.

11. Stone, *Christian Messenger* 13 (October, 1843): 165.

12. Carisse Mickey Berryhill, "Alexander Campbell's Natural Rhetoric of Evangelism," *Restoration Quarterly* 30 (1980): 124.

13. Andrew Bart Wall, "A Study of Disaffiliation from Churches of Christ in Southern California" (Ph.D. dissertation, Fuller Theological Seminary, 2001), 1.

14. Moses Lard, "The Reformation for Which We Plead," *Lard's Quarterly* (September 1963): 18-22.

15. Hughes, "How Barton Stone Led Me," 177.

CPSIA information can be obtained at www.ICGtesting.com
Printed in the USA
LVOW062038050712

288808LV00004B/2/P